The BLACK FLOWER

STORIES, POEMS, AND PITHY SAYINGS OF

GLEN ALFRED HARRIS

EDITOR AND INTRODUCTION
BY
LYNN HARRIS REGUDON

The Black Flower: Stories, Poems And Pithy Sayings Of Glen Alfred Harris © 2022 Lynn Harris Regudon

All rights reserved. With the exception of short excerpts used in critical review, no part of this work may be reproduced, transmitted, or stored in any form whatsoever, without the prior written permission of the publisher. Creation, exploitation, and distribution of any unauthorized editions of this work, in any format in existence now or in the future—including but not limited to text, audio, and video—is prohibited without the prior written permission of the publisher.

Publishing services provided by Archangel Ink | archangelink.com

Paperback ISBN: 978-1-950043-48-4

*For my brothers, Glen Jr. and
Trevor, sons of our father,
Glen A. Harris, Sr.
And
Our combined children:
John, Mark, Trevor Todd,
Nish, Lisa and Garth*

In Memory of Glen Alfred Harris

Contents

Introduction 1

Short Stories

A Visionary Gleam 16

A Silhouette of Burma 19

The Black Flower 24

A Test of Nerves 38

Otto 43

The Wager 48

Basements and Bargains 53

They That Be Slain By The Sword 57

The Forest Pool 97

Poems

Sonnet (Evening Fantasy) 100

Sonnet (Man and Life) 101

Sonnet (Peace is Best) 102

Sonnet (To Psyche—Absent) 103

Sonnet (To Psyche) 104

Sonnet (Futility) 105

Sonnet (En Passant) 106

The Unredeemed 107

Untitled 1-9	111
Slow Stain	117
Subliminal	118
Waterfront	119
To A Pretty Waitress	120
To A Good Neighbor (Mr. Moore at 93)	121
To Roslyn and Glen Jr. at 50 Lines	122
Beholden	123
Forbearance	124
A Christmas Prayer	125
A Commission	126
A Golden Parting	127
A Petition	128
A Thought For......	129
An Impression	130
Argument	131
A Wish	133
At The Ritz	134
Birthday Thoughts	135
Broken Dream	136
Christmas Cheer	137
Could I But Know	139
Culture—Modern Style	140
Dinner a la Tacoma	141

For Flossie	142
En Passant (To Flossie)	143
In Aureum Memoriam (To Flossie)	144
Ghosts	145
Inheritance	146
Last Words	147
Lesson	149
Lines for ---	150
Lines To A Stye	152
Lines to Marion	154
Love	155
My 'Friendly' Neighbor	156
Nocturne	158
Nocturne and Awakening	159
Prelude	160
Reflections of an Un-Naturalist – The Crossbill	162
Requiem for F.R.H. (After Tagore)	163
Song	164
To Vilda	165
To A Baby, Growing	167
Song for Music (On Puget Sound)	168
Sonnet 1, 2	169
Sonnet To----	171
Sonnet To Beauty	172

Spring Nocturne In Seattle 173

Spring Nostalgia 175

Spring Song 176

Strictly Academic 177

Summer Treasure 178

The Brownies 179

The Graduate 181

The Gobbler's Lament (For Thanksgiving) 182

The Last Avatar (of Vishnu) 184

The Nothing Book Speaks 185

The Prisoner 186

The Woman Speaks 187

To the Little Mite 189

Ultima Thule 190

What's In A Name? 192

Wood 194

Limericks, One-Liners And Other Nonsense 195

Acknowledgements 209

Cover Biography 211

Introduction

Glen Harris sits at the dining room table, a sly, secretive smile twitching at the corners of his mouth. This instructor of freshman English, surrounded by the evidences of his profession, delicately takes a small pad and a pen from an old cheese glass. The well-used coffee cup and saucer, with drips of sugar and cream, are in front of the placemat next to an equally well-used ashtray. A pile of student papers, partially graded, occupies one side atop the *Harbrace Handbook*. On the other side, a short stack of library books awaits opening. I have been around him long enough to recognize the signs: something, perhaps a one-liner or a pithy phrase, for which we know him well, is about to be born. At the other end of the table, his wife, Florence (Flossie to friends and family), instructor in the Psychology Preschool Laboratory at the University of Washington, maintains her own somewhat smaller individualistic piles. It is a picture that remains one of my favorite memories.

It is my intent to put all my father's writings together in one place, to make them available and preserve them especially for the family, but also for anyone else who may find his writings interesting, amusing, or poignant. The few writings that have been published were at a time when he was an undergraduate or graduate student, and those primarily in university publications. I have indicated the publishing sources and dates of these. I have separated all into three categories, with an attempt to put the prose in chronological order whenever possible; the poetry somewhat alphabetical, with dates where known. I have not edited any of his writing unless it was to update spellings from some of his more nineteenth-century British styles—a challenge, given his penchant for long, obscure, and made-up words. I have not changed those. But the quality of the writing speaks for itself, and many of the limericks and one-liners should bring a smile to the reader's lips. A brief biography of his life, which follows, may provide the reader with the context of his writing.

Glen Alfred Harris was born in Dharwar, Bombay Presidency, India on March 10, 1899. Glen was the second of four children. The oldest was Ruby, born two years before. Following Glen's birth, his brother Ramsay Jr. made his appearance, and several years later, after a move to Burma, the youngest member, Pansy, was born.

Glen's father, Ramsay Alfred Gooch Harris, Sr., also born in India, did office work for a railway company in Dharwar until 1902, when the family moved to Bangalore in south India. There Ramsay Sr. taught English at the Episcopalian Bishop Cotton School. The family lived in a brick house called Gowrian Lodge. Its high ceilings and an open flagstone porch helped mitigate the tropical heat. The yard was filled with fruit trees: papaya, mango, soursop and guava. A drumstick tree's long beans provided one ingredient for the daily curries. Indoor plumbing was not an option.

In 1907, Ramsay Sr. was recruited to teach English at a school for native Burmese children in Minbu, Burma (now Myanmar). His children, however, were not allowed to attend the native school, and there was no other school where they could be enrolled. It was a period of educational limbo for Glen, Ramsay Jr. and Ruby, but the three made diligent use of the local library and read widely. Though not mentioned in correspondence or other writings, doubtless some home schooling took place.

The family lived in a succession of four houses in Minbu, on the banks of the Irrawaddy River. The first was a wooden and mat house right on the edge of the river, elevated three feet off the ground, to protect against the monsoon flooding. The second house was built on pillars for the same reason even though it was three-quarters of a mile away from the river. It was here that the youngest child, Pansy, was born. This house was also mat-walled with a thatch roof. Even here the flood waters rose up into the yard. Glen and Ramsay Jr. told of floating around in zinc bathtubs! Although their mother was terrified of the water and tried to keep them away from it, they had learned to swim on the sly by the time they got to high school.

The third and fourth residences were more substantial, the last in a wing of the school where Ramsay Sr. taught, even though the children were still not allowed to attend.

At that time there were no other English families in Minbu. The Indian Civil Service (ICS) which ran the country were men, the "cream of the intellectuals," and brought English snobbery with them. If one were born in India, as was Ramsay Sr., even though of English parents, he was not allowed into the clubs. If married to a native woman, like their next door neighbor, he would be snubbed altogether. With these societal restrictions, Ramsay's children had no other English children with whom to play, so they played with the native children. These social attitudes made an impression on Glen and his siblings, manifesting more as resistance to the prejudices. With Glen, however, a tiny bit of the old Colonial British snobbery persisted. Mingling with the native children, and exposure to the native languages, however, gave them a closer understanding of the culture than some of the "elites."

Glen spoke often of the great respect they had for C.W. Ainley, the principal of the native school where his father taught in Minbu. It was this man who engineered Ramsay's transfer to Maymyo in 1912, to teach in the Government High School for boys where Ramsay Jr. and

Glen could finally attend school. Ruby and Pansy went to Anglican church schools, St. Michael's and All Angels.

In Maymyo, Glen got his start with the two things he became proud of in later life: music and gymnastics. He acquired his first tiny bamboo flute, and also a piccolo, mail-ordered from Bombay.

He told me how he learned to walk on his hands, and would be regarded with amazement, as he "walked" down the street, feet in the air. Indeed, the few pictures I saw of my father before we met were of him standing on his hands in some unlikely place—atop my grandparents roof, or a cannon in a park.

A look at the daily routine gives a glimpse of what life was like for Glen and his family. Water was brought daily by "water-wallas" (water merchants) in huge leather bags called *mashuks,* and emptied into large earthenware containers called *jumlars,* which kept the water cool. Servants did the cooking and cleaning. Mother decided on the menu, and the cook went to market each day—there was no refrigeration. All families had a curry stone, a rectangular piece of granite especially chipped, and a granite roller, on which the cook ground spices in a little water for daily use. (After the Burmese cook was discovered to have syphilis or leprosy [sources differ on which disease it was], he was sent away, and Glen's mother and her sister, Mabel, took over that job.) The kitchen was separate from the house, with a wood-burning fireplace and its own roof. Oil lamps were the source of light after dark.

The family had an upright piano in Maymyo, which their mother played. Glen took flute lessons from Professor Rampazotti, obtaining a more sophisticated six-keyed flute. The love for this instrument followed him all his life, and a great many family memories centered around his playing at home, and in camp sites.

Glen joined the Boy Scouts while in Burma, playing his piccolo on marches. His soccer and tennis games improved, and with more equipment available, he became quite expert in gymnastics. When he graduated from The Government High School for Europeans in 1918, his certificate notes that he had a "special aptitude for music and athletics," and that his "health and physique" were "both excellent."

Churches were a source of social life in the "Colonies" and although the Anglican church was the British offshoot, Glen described the priest in Maymyo as a "fat, oleaginous heel" who was not well-liked. With the Baptist church having a more active social agenda, the family attended there, a serendipitous choice. In 1916, a missionary from the United States arrived in the person of Dr. Stanley Baldwin. This event became a game-changer in the lives of the Ramsay Harris family.

Dr. Baldwin befriended the Harris boys, often inviting them on hikes around the area. His church in New Jersey sent him $500 to buy an automobile for his use, but with the prohibitive price of gasoline, and roads better suited to oxen and horse carts, he sought permission of his church to use the money to send the boys to Colgate University in upstate New York, his own alma mater. After a year in Rangoon College, the boys returned to Maymyo, and Dr. Baldwin persuaded them to take him up on his offer. They arrived in Hamilton, New York, home of Colgate University, in September, 1920, and a new world opened up for them.

The more egalitarian atmosphere was a new experience, and both young men reveled in it. To augment their meager budgets, they both found part-time jobs of a type that would have been unthinkable in Burma. Glen learned how to maintain the heating system of the boarding house in which he lived after he moved out of the dormitories. He also worked in a box factory nearby for at least one summer.

Both Glen and Ramsay wrote music and lyrics for Colgate-inspired songs that were played at Colgate long after they left. Glen played his beloved flute, too, in the university orchestra.

The professors lauded by Dr. Baldwin measured up to his high praise. Dr. Crawshaw, who taught literature, was one of Glen's favorites.

It was this man to whom he gave credit for steering him into a life of teaching English writing and literature.

Glen had had little experience with women in Burma—the caste/class system had obviated that. There were seldom "suitable" young women, except for the wives of British officials, with whom to associate. It was considered déclassé to associate with native girls. But here in America, girls were of more equal stature, and among the local young women, Glen found the one who became his first wife, Helen Palmer. He married her at the time of his graduation in 1923.

Following graduation, he taught for a year at Syracuse University, then moved to Redlands, California, where he taught at Redlands University. It was here that we two girls were born, Vilda in 1927, and I in 1929.

Just a few months after I was born, the marriage fell apart and my mother moved back to Hamilton with me, leaving my sister, disabled by spastic paraplegia, with her father, at his insistence. In my mother's mind, it was to be a brief separation, but it proved to be permanent. Vilda ultimately was cared for by her grandparents, until her death in 1953, at age 26.

Shortly after our departure, Glen got into some trouble with the university, a Baptist organization, for "fraternizing" (whatever that meant) with one or more of his female students, who was "not his wife," and they fired him. Without a job, a wife and daughter who had separated from him, and a disabled daughter who needed a lot of care, he sold his house and moved in with his parents. (Ramsay Jr. had brought them over from Burma and had bought them a house in Redlands.) Assured that Vilda would receive the loving care she needed from her grandparents, Glen moved to Seattle, Washington, to pursue his PhD at the University of Washington.

As a graduate student, he managed his tuition and living expenses with a small stipend by teaching freshman English. It was in one of his classes that he met Florence Ring, blond, blue-eyed and highly intelligent. It didn't take long for them to solidify their relationship and they moved in together, an unusual choice in the early 1930s.

Here the history becomes somewhat unclear. After her graduation, Florence, an education major, taught elementary school in Cashmere, a small town in eastern Washington. At the time, married women were not allowed to teach public school in Washington. Like many others during those early years of the Great Depression, Glen lost his job at the University in 1932. Glen Jr. was born two years later, and by then they were back in Seattle. Junior was quickly nicknamed Trog to distinguish him from his father. (Trog, from troglodyte, reflected the cave-like house they lived in when he was born, so Glen Sr. told me.)

Sometime during this period, Glen and Flossie did home demonstrations of a cookware called Guardian Service, similar to the "parties" in individual's homes given today to promote a product. In the early 1930's, Glen also had a radio program called "Mary's Friendly Garden" which was said to have drawn a devoted audience.

Money was always in short supply but generally there was enough to pay rent and feed the family. Then in 1937, Flossie entered a limerick contest for the Amos 'n' Andy radio program. She won $1,500, which was a small fortune for that time. That started a trend, and they entered many such contests over the years, and won a number of prizes. (One of the last ones that Flossie entered yielded a flatiron. She was incensed! "I already have one of those!")

In 1938, their youngest son, Trevor, was born.

During the early 1940's, Glen worked as a draftsman for Webster-Brinkley, a Department of Defense contractor, where his marital relationship came under scrutiny. Management there gave him an ultimatum: marry the woman you are living with or you will be fired. Since he now had two children with the woman who had been his unofficial wife for all those years, they promptly married, and his job was secure.

In March of 1945, he made a break from Webster-Brinkley's

demanding 10-hour days, and returned to finish his PhD at the University of Washington, and teach freshman English again. Flossie, by this time, was a graduate assistant working toward her own Master's, teaching at the Psychology Preschool Laboratory at the University of Washington. With their income finally stabilized, they bought a house across from Ravenna Park in the University District.

With both teaching at the University, vacation times now coordinated, the family spent the summers exploring the Northwest, visiting relatives in Montana and California, and camping along the way.

A small, but important event occurred on January 28, 1946: Glen Alfred Harris, Sr. became an American citizen, after twenty-six years in the country.

Then in July of 1947, at the age of seventeen, I met my father for the first time since my mother had taken me away. This memorable reunion took place at the Seattle-Tacoma International airport, when I arrived from Hamilton, New York, where I had grown up with my mother and stepfather. I fell in love immediately with this handsome man of forty-seven, black hair graying at the temples, of medium height and appearing quite fit. My new stepmother, Flossie, was first to welcome me, with open arms. My father, nattily dressed in a tweed suit, white shirt and dark tie, gave me a welcoming hug, and the sixteen plus years since he had last seen me vanished for both of us. Then he introduced my two younger half-brothers, Glen Jr., (Trog) age thirteen, and Trevor, age nine. I did not meet my older sister, Vilda, until later in that year, when he took me to spend Christmas with my paternal grandparents in Redlands, California, with whom she had lived since the age of two. Over the ensuing years, my father's story would gradually become fleshed out by him and this new family of mine, and also with the help of his brother, Ramsay, Jr. and his family.

By 1952, Glen had still not completed his PhD. All the testing was done, orals and written, but he had run into a kerfuffle over the topic of his thesis. His choice was Rabindranath Tagore, but the chair of his thesis committee did not allow it because "no one in the Department could critique it." Although he started to work on his assigned subject, he lost heart, and did not complete the thesis by the deadline, so they let him go.

Casting about for work, and recognizing that his gift of gab had worked well for him over the years, he got a job as salesman for a roofing materials company called Panther. It was a traveling job and he made a reasonable living from it. Although he never did the roofing applications himself, one summer he recruited his two young sons, Glen, Jr. home from Yale, and Trevor, a junior in high school, to apply the tar-like material on the roof of the Presbyterian Church in the University District. Both remember that job with considerably less than glee.

Other jobs around that time included with a company called Colotile, another with a company that produced frozen foods, and Pacific Engineering where he wrote procedures.

Young Trevor graduated from high school in 1956, and immediately got a job at Boeing Aircraft. It did not take long before Glen realized his son was making more money than he ever had, so he decided to apply at Boeing, too. They hired him as a technical writer, which suited his personality well, and made good use of his writing skills. He loved the interviews with other employees done in the performance of his job, and remained there until Boeing, typical of its pattern, included him in one of its massive lay-offs just three months before he could have retired with full pension in 1964, at age 65.

By this time, Flossie was the director of the Psychology Laboratory Preschool, so their income was stable. Their summers were often spent driving the open roads, camping, and collecting rocks, which provided Glen with a new hobby of cutting and polishing rocks for fun, not much for profit.

These are the *facts* of Glen Harris's growing up and adulthood, but what was he like as a person? Flossie described him in her first letter to me as "a kind and loving father…even-tempered, humorous, with a wealth of patience and understanding." I have to agree with her assessment, but there was more than those simple attributes.

He was definitely a ladies man, drawn to the fair sex particularly if she were intelligent. He could regale his friends and the young women with quotes from poets, Shakespeare, and a myriad of authors. His memory for literature was prodigious. Once he caught a student plagiarizing from an obscure African author the student thought his instructor could not possibly have read. On the student's paper, Glen made note of the title of the book and the chapter from which the passage was lifted, and the young fellow earned himself a low grade.

Dishonesty, whether in such a nonthreatening way as plagiarism, or in business, was unacceptable to him. Trevor got himself into trouble with his father on one occasion. He and a friend had strolled into a drugstore on the way home from grade school one day. The friend, a kid with street smarts, suggested they jimmy the gumball machine. They were successful and Trevor took his prize, but his conscience got the better of him and he told his father. Glen immediately took him back to the drugstore and made him confess to his misdeed, which he did, tearfully. It was a lesson Trevor never forgot, in part because of the utter humiliation of having to confess. (It engendered a life-long aversion toward attempting to cheat in any way.)

Glen readily made friends. The librarians of the University Branch Library knew him by first name when he made his weekly visit to exchange books. He read widely on all kinds of subjects, and was always interested in astronomy and the planets, later becoming a member of the Planetary Society after retirement. I cannot recall a day when he did not have a book in front of him, wherever he was sitting—different ones for different places. His eclectic reading habits led him to introduce his young son, Glen Jr. (Trog) to the world of dinosaurs at a very early age, which blossomed into a life-long love of those extinct creatures. At his retirement party, Trog's colleagues made special mention of his memos to his staff resplendent with hand-drawn dinosaurs, which they dubbed Dino-Memos.

Another pastime was drawing. Father introduced me to three-part drawings, in which one person would draw the head, fold over the paper with lines drawn to start the body, and fold again, lines drawn, to draw the legs, each part done by a different person who did not see what the one before him had drawn. Trog and Trevor were equally skilled at this task, but with very different styles, and the results were often quite amazing—and weird. I did not have their talent but tried anyway. Among Glen's favorite subjects were leprechauns, and side margins of class notes and letters were often populated by the wee people and/or their habitat.

Glen was a firm believer in the beauty of the human body, and saw no reason to cover it up at home. He—and indeed, the whole family—often would be found wandering around the house in the morning without a stitch, except that Glen always wore socks and shoes. Sometimes that was all he wore when he went into the back yard, which I'm sure amused (maybe embarrassed) neighbors on both sides of him. I confess the first morning I spent there, that was a bit of a shock, coming from a firm New England upbringing. I do recall one time being the first to arrive in a campsite in Eastern Washington, everyone disrobed (except for shoes and socks, of course). Not long afterward, another carload of campers arrived, took one look, and turned around and left. That camp we had all to ourselves! (Nudity was not a choice when we happened on a campsite already populated.)

By the early 1970s, finally being empty-nesters, they had the freedom to do whatever they wished. Flossie retired around 1974, and their camping trips became longer and reached farther. In the winter, they took up bowling with a seniors group.

Then in 1980, I received a frantic call from my father about 2 a.m.

to tell me he couldn't wake Flossie and he was afraid she was dead. I dressed immediately and went to the house, called 911, and it was the emergency medical technician who confirmed her death and called the coroner. The coroner was legally responsible for people dying at home or outside a hospital. Because it was felt to be of natural causes, the coroner agreed to forego autopsy, and allow her body to be taken by the University Medical School, where she had willed it. Glen did not want a funeral or memorial service; I think in some ways that gave him no closure. I tried to be with him as often as I could, but by then, I was divorced, raising two children on my own, and working two jobs, so my presence was spotty.

Glen did adjust, doing his own cooking, cleaning (rarely), and kept up with bowling for a little while, quitting after he had twisted his back in an awkward maneuver.

After that, he was mostly alone, except for one interval when he met a young woman who asked to rent a room from him while her house was being renovated. This went on for a time, even getting him to the point where he thought he might ask her to marry him. But she clearly was looking at him more as a father-figure than a potential mate, for she married a few months later.

Without his roommate, he fell back into contests in earnest. "I'd like to win a million before I die," he said to me once, and to that end regularly bought all manner of things from Reader's Digest, and Publishers Clearing House, to the point where boxes cluttered every room. When narrow pathways to the bathroom and kitchen were all that was left, new arrivals were thrown into the basement, or piled on the stairs to the second floor, which was now unused. He would open a box once in awhile, as a "Christmas present" to himself.

Though he managed to pay his bills and had enough to buy groceries, he spent a great deal of money over time, and rarely won anything. He refused to let me balance his checkbook, mostly, I think, because he didn't want me to see how much he was spending on "chance."

By this time he was really deaf, not just "conveniently" so. Trevor had him fitted for hearing aides but he seldom wore them, even managing to step on one and break it, which both of us thought he did on purpose. He hated admitting his deafness, at first even hiding the dry-erase board I got for communicating with him. His hearing issues also proved a problem for the phone. He could barely hear voices and tended to say yes to anything that sounded like a question. His live-in "girlfriend" had thwarted one scam, and I likely had thwarted another when the phone rang once while I was there. But he never heard the burglar who came into his house after he had gone to bed (about 5 a.m.) and made off with his car and blank checks. The car was the biggest blow, because it was his freedom. (We kids, however, were eternally grateful, because his driving had deteriorated along with his hearing.) It took quite a while to clear that one up.

When he was 101, he started falling, always backwards, and frequently hitting his head. After several such instances, I came by one afternoon on my way to my evening job to find him lying under the dining room table in his dressing gown. When he saw me, he said, "Now, Lynnie, tell me—what are these structures?" and pointed to the table legs. I immediately called 911, and we got him to the emergency room of the hospital where I worked. He was diagnosed with a subdural hematoma, and was admitted to the Neurology Intensive Care Unit, drifting in and out of consciousness. After a week or so he stabilized, but it was obvious he could no longer manage on his own, so he was discharged to a nursing home north of Seattle. He never left there, and died at the age of 107, having announced to his niece the night before that he was going to die that night. Uncanny how that can work.

So ended the long, mostly happy life of the Glen A. Harris, Sr., who wrote the stories, poems and one-liners herein.

Lynn Harris Regudon

Short Stories

A Visionary Gleam

(Written at Rangoon College, Rangoon, Burma,
probably at age 19 or 20)

With a sigh of relief I threw my pen down, infinitely rejoiced to have at length completed my work; and pushing back my chair I rose and glanced out of my window and marked the grotesque lengthening of the shadows, the luxuriously rich orange beams of the sun which softly kissed the peaceful, drowsy countryside to sleep, and away to where "the great high priest in his garments resplendent" seemed as though poised in sacerdotal majesty for a space before he should suddenly plunge down and vanish beneath the far horizon at the signal of the sunset gun. Truly was the prospect passing fair to gaze upon, and the mellow beauty conspiring with the time of day all but succeeded in snapping meditative bracelets on me. But I was aware that if I wished to repair to my favourite nook hard by the lake adjacent to the house, in order to snatch a few delightful minutes with the Muse, I would have to make haste. So I stepped to the mahogany bookcase and letting my glance stray over the gilt backs, selected a volume and drew it out. This drawing out of books was a source of constant delight to me for it gave me a never-failing thrill to feel the soft covers and to hear the luxurious swish of the pale blue silk binding as a volume left its companions. And now as I strayed down the sloping track and turned off at the little side path with soft steps I became acutely aware of the mystery which lurked, whispering among the somber shadows of the denser thickets, conscious of a latent benign influence in this vesper scene steeped in "the silence and the calm of mute insensate" things. A bird whirred suddenly away with rude clamour, an inconsistency which dispersed the gathering mists of dreaming, and I walked on and sank down on the great hollowed out stone set against the massive trunk of a forest giant and arranged myself in the most comfortably negligent posture—I confess to being an epicure of a peculiar order—and suffered my volume to fall open at random. I read. Now here was a strange antithesis to my present surroundings, for the lines ran:

"....the sun sprang forth
Rejoicing in his splendour, and the
Mask Of darkness fell from the awakened
Earth."

What a vivid vision I thought that presented, a vision of surpassing brilliance, one whose constituent tone colours conjoined to form a perfect whole. A marvelously lucid expression of thought and maturity of conception. And yet!—And yet! Only thirty summers flew over his head! Far over the lake among the distant deepening shadows of the opposite shores my eyes rested, ideas, thoughts coursing through my mind in a chaotic whirl. But what was this? What now? The chaos was resolving itself and the lake sank away and a new vista presented itself. I looked and a spacious Elysian prospect passed slowly in panoramic changes; but there in the centre, a scene of transcendent beauty arrested my regard. Who are those white-stoled figures standing before that great throne-altar as though in rapt adoration? Gradually the scene became clearer and its import dawned upon me; for now I see the form seated on the great throne clad in wondrous raiment with a helm of burnished gold; at her side is a sparkling fount and there are those around to whom she is ministering with its waters in greater or less degree. Many received of her and at last those to whom She bestowed faded and passed away; and a great throng in dazzling white radiance came forward and I specially note "one frale Form" standing a little apart, companionless. And here it was suddenly borne in upon my understanding that this semblance of divinity was the Muse of all the Ages. One by one she calls and blesses her servants till only he who is remote from the throng is left; she sees him, a glorious smile of love wreathes her countenance and beckoning to him she fervently blesses and stooping down kisses him. He rose. I saw that his was the beauty of a woman and his lips were stained with love. And the Muse of all the Ages waved her hand, "Pass thou along," she said, "thou best philosopher—thou who has served me best and hearkened to my every whisper." And he moved away along a way strown with "a light of laughing flowers." The wonderful picture slowly dissolved as a I looked and there again was the lake trembling to the last caress of a long golden shaft slanting along its surface. Another shaft glanced on the open page in my hand and I read "he, as I guess, had gazed on Nature's naked loveliness" and I became conscious that he who said "He is made one with Nature" is the only truly, intensely real bard of all time.

A Silhouette of Burma

(Published in the *Willow Path* at Colgate University about 1921)

Heavens! Did I ever tell you how Chumley—but there, I must not anticipate. Order is one of the laws of heaven (at least I have been told that, I don't know); but Chumley, if you had told him that, would have looked at you vaguely and wondered where the analogy came in. You see, Chumley's life was rather—but wait, I implore, I'm anticipating again.... What I wanted to tell you at first was that Chumley's present lot in life, besides the half-acre he ruled, was to nurse a baby—and a grudge. He never told me what the object of the latter was, but that, of course, neither mattered nor altered my suspicions. I know he often "shoo-ed" the baby at unhallowed hours of the night, while that impish animal (I use Chumley's own phrase) brayed stentorian objections. He often told us in hushed confidence, and with unsuspected heat, that there were only two things which proved really insupportable to him—namely, Minbu and life. We pointedly assured him that it would be the simplest thing, if he so desired, to free himself of both curses (with the tacit and bold assumption that he privately spelled life with a "w".) On that head, however, Chumley was a tomb. But Trix (who, though young, is surprisingly positive about most things) was willing to take her judicial oath on it. For a whole week after that particular tête-à-tête I was disturbed into unhappy reflections on Freudian "complexes" and "inferiorities", which carried me to a remote and unused section of the public library. Daws, the official custodian of books, gaped hugely at this neurotic streak, and, being a thorough-going idiot of unquestioned parts, shook his head, scratched it reflectively—and gave it up (I mean, of course, the problem). Freud was likewise a tomb, and yielded not a jot. I finally came to the conclusion, in regard to Chumley's declaration, that he had unhappily lighted upon a synonym for "life" wholly unsuspected by Roget when compiling his comprehensive *Thesaurus*. I refrained, however, from mentioning my discovery to Chumley; you see, he might have eyed my philology with rank suspicion.

It frequently happened, when ghosting of Oxford days out on my verandah, that Chumley came to the end of a cigarette and his patience at the same moment. At such times, being burdened, he became quite frank and swore he was bored by the East—specifically and in general. It only later got out that such outbursts always followed a particularly savage and sanguine encounter with hordes of bloodthirsty mosquitoes. I learned to appreciate his phrase.

I distinctly remember a single night spent at Chumley's bungalow. At one in the morning, when the night was growing old and the morning young, I awoke to find the air still and sultry. There was every kind of evidence (chiefly damning) to know that the night was populous with mosquitoes. I smiled in the darkness, and snuggling down in my bed felt bold and defiant towards the thirsty horde without, securely entrenched behind my curtain. I thought of Chumley sleeping like a babe behind the partition, unprotected against the enemy, and marveled at such consummate arrogance.

Just as I began to doze off again, Chumley stirred…awoke. I could hear that. I remember I wondered vaguely what he would do now. He informed me himself pretty soon. Brushing his face with his hand, he turned over, and daringly prepared to take a new lease of deep and liquid rest. There was actually silence for a whole minute. I listened the wheeling squadrons and their incessant battle-cries, and thankfully regarded my own lot as God-given. But suddenly, when I had but reached the goal of oblivion, Chumley lashed out in the darkness, breaking both the partition and the silence. Wide awake now, I concluded a marauding band had camped for the nonce on his face to play backgammon, sip newly tapped nectar, and generally indulge in gastronomic obscenities. Apparently physical force only called forth the mockery of his assailants, for they returned to the charge with recruited forces, shrieking derisively in his very ear, and jabbing him viciously in the most unexpected quarters. Thoroughly aroused by this, he was defending himself heroically against these frontal and flank attacks, but with little credit to himself.

Chumley became dangerous; he likewise became voluble and unprintable in the same breath, showering imprecations and blows on the void, hitting the partition, the bed post, and (I admit to my shame) my sense of humor! All at once he hurled discretion and a book to the winds (the latter with unpremeditated dexterity as it described an arc over the partition and whizzed by my head), and for a few minutes went berserk and played a part "fit to tear a cat, and make all split!" The night became a perfect revel of chromatic insubordination! He became the veriest fish-wife, slapping, abusing, and indulging everything that was primitive. I was frankly astounded at Chumley's agility with uncanonized idiom; I never knew he had it in him. Finally, in pure desperation, he played the hedgehog and retired beneath his coverings. In the morning, at *chota hazri* or breakfast, he invoked all the demigods that ever trod Lethean strands to witness his resolution to sleep under a curtain or suffocate.

Chumley was no Philomath; he even admitted it unasked. His private life (as I hinted before) was not made of the stuff which insinuated heaven; in fact, quite the reverse. But he derived a fleeting pleasure from assiduously exploring the recesses of a tenth-rate Parnassus. His pursuits in this field would certainly have qualified him for a glorified place in a mutual admiration society; for he hobnobbed, when he felt leisurely and indolent, with a whole shelf of lewd fellows who had made it their business to gabble in verse. They had attained, had "drunk deep" with spluttering lips at some, as yet, undiscovered "Pierian

Spring", were therefore in print (also 'out of print', as I learned later), and were therefore impeccable. But Chumley did not stop there. He composed! At the inspiration of a tenth muse, his pen transfixed every vagrant fancy that dared to show a leg and set it to foolscap. And from a more than hand-shaking acquaintance with these yawpists, these banjo-thrummers in poetry, these retired colonels who had eschewed the barrack-room and the sword for the ballad-room and the pen, Chumley himself had acquired a fashion of the pen that was highly discomposing, to say the least, to the type of temperament generally associated with haggard editors and frantic press reporters. Backed by his lisping coterie he invested the editorial office of the *Rangoon Gazette* and demanded a place in the ranks of the penny-a-liners. But from the start it was plainly apparent that the Muse of numbers had never passed that way, and Chumley's correspondence became vocal with official "regrets"—with frequent and degenerate variations on the same theme. Only on one solitary occasion did Chumley register a score—and then it was morally certain that the editorial *chevaux-de-frise* was down during a lightning thrust!

It came to my notice one evening as I reclined on my verandah. Before me stretched the twilight-glimmer of the Irrawaddy in flood, flecked by an occasional paddy-boat which steered slowly through masses of floating driftwood. It was an hour calculated to suggest peace and repose. Mingled with the musical tinkle of pagoda bells, however, there was wafted in from mid-stream the syncopated strains of a Burmese pastoral ditty, rendered with amazing volume and scant good taste by some daring swain clinging, leech-like, to a flood-time derelict which was apparently as buoyant as his spirits. From this composite setting I harked back to one mystical moment to draw an obscure parallel with one "lowing herd" of my school-day recitations. Thus idly musing, I be-thought me of the local herds of bilious-looking "byles" (cattle), and turned again in disgust to my paper.

Steeling myself against the mendicant array of over- solicitous headlines, declamatory of everything from murders to the jaundiced ethics of the *gymkhana*, I glanced casually through until my attention became suddenly riveted at the bottom of the poet's corner.

"Chumley"—I read…blinked…read again.

Personally, I like poetry. I was always in full agreement that poetry, like politics, has its conventions, but you would never get Chumley to acknowledge the restraint of convention. Its amenities simply had no significance for him. Melody, rhythm, and common sense were one and all at each other's throats. Chumley's muse, in a word, walked the land pipeless, arrogant, and goat-footed, voluble, shameless, and abusive.

For months thereafter Chumley was stalked by the specter of the sylvan maid who, having decided to abjure the delights of her Sabine farm for the lights of the city, came to the metropolis and conceived a violent

"Passion for clam chowder
And some lang'rous scented powder."

I believe that Chumley is still out there in the East, but as for me, I have long ago come to the conclusion that Soho is more conducive to aesthetics than the teeming life of Burma—with Minbu, mosquitoes, and Chumley!

The Black Flower

At nine o'clock on a moonless night a high-powered motorcycle leapt through the west gate of the great Fort in Mandalay. It roared up the lonely street at dangerous speed. The single headlight stabbed the darkness, swept across the gloom like a meteor. Roadside objects jumped into grotesque focus, reared up like startled monsters, then toppled back into the engulfing night. But the hurrying, apparently reckless rider, wearing the smart official uniform of the Mandalay Police, stared only at the lighted ribbon of road. A deep frown divided his brows.

Seldom had Swithinbanks been faced with so grave a problem as that which had arisen suddenly, in the late afternoon, within the sacred precincts of the Arakan Pagoda. As Commissioner of Police for Mandalay District, he was beset with the urgency for swift official action. Any bungling, he knew, would lead to a general flare-up among the fanatical priesthood. The Brass Hats would squint down their noses and hint the Empire was going to pot, and the air about the clubs would be charged with brimstone for a season.

"Blasted devilry!" he gritted. "And I warned that young fool Prendergast…"

Hurtling along the road, he reviewed the facts, probing them carefully for a cause. Prendergast, a sub fresh from England, larded with public school swagger and importance, had drawn upon himself the dark baptism meted out to all foolhardy offenders against the inscrutable gods. For a moment, Swithinbanks pictured the scene: Prendergast angrily pushing past native guards and stalking up that long dim aisle to the sacred Turtle Tank, ignoring the Buddhist rite of treading hallowed ground unshod. Then the guard's signal to the priests: the high silver note of a gong, struck once. The unsuspecting officer suddenly swept into a nightmare struggle, in which, with devilish dispatch, the yellow-robed ones deprived him of nose and ears and ejected him from the north gate, a pitiful and ruinous object.

The speeding Commissioner, skimming these facts critically, felt more lurked behind the affair than a moment's offense, something farther afield of which this was the grim herald. He knew the subtle interlocking that bound the priesthood into a well-knit fraternity, whose outposts stretched away to the remotest villages in the hills.

In the hills...

Suddenly, like the flash and crack of a completed circuit, he had the solution to the problem. He had almost forgotten the two American scientists who had dined with him two months ago and then quietly disappeared into the Shan Hills in quest of a strange black flower. Professor Stanton and his friend, Cyrus P. Hottinger, had somewhere heard a trickle of rumor about this flower, a sacred flower, they claimed, that was black and of extraordinary size. Maybe, the Commissioner thought skeptically, but it sounded by poppycock, bizarre as travelers' tales. But if it was a <u>sacred</u> flower, there was bound to be a mess with the priests. What did these scientific johnnies expect, anyway? A hand-out from the holy-of-holies? Or were blood and violence to be the twin harbingers of this venture? If so, what of the two Americans?

It was odd, the Commissioner reflected much later, how the tangible answers to all his questions were thrust at him that night. For all at once he found himself rushing upon a huddle of brown, scantily clad figures swaying together, tearing at something in their midst. A great *dah* flashed aloft and fell. He cut his motor, snatched at his Webley and zipped a bullet over their heads as the heavy machine coasted up. Instantly the natives scattered, ducking out of the glare. As he vaulted from the saddle, Swithinbanks caught the swirl of a yellow robe vanishing into the gloom. The victim of the attack sprawled in the dust at his feet, and Swithinbanks saw that he was a Hindu wearing the uniform of a government telegraph runner. His turban was gone. Blood poured from a long gash across his shaved head.

"Ai-eee—sahib!" he gasped weakly, still clutching his leather telegram case. "The pigs of pagoda-folk—the message for the sahib!" He tried to rise.

"No, lie still." Swithinbanks quickly pocketed the case. He tore a strip from the man's turban and roughly bandaged the wound, keenly aware that eyes watched from the darkness. "You did well. It will be remembered."

Even as he spoke he heard the clop-clop of hoofs and saw the two yellow lamps of an approaching *gharri*. The carriage was empty and without delay he lifted the injured man in.

"To the hospital!"

The frightened driver whipped up the single pony and was gone as the Commissioner's motor roared again.

In the dining room of his white bungalow Swithinbanks thoughtfully sipped a whiskey and soda. Before him lay the telegram which he pondered with knit brows. The message was brief, startling:

ARRIVE NINE-FIFTY TRAIN STOP STAYING OVERNIGHT STOP SECURED SPECIMEN BLACK FLOWER STOP WHOOPEE

C.P. Hottinger

The boastful indiscretion of it shocked and annoyed Swithinbanks. Did the two Americans hold themselves somehow exempt from the curious decrees of the East, where the dark man's knife is whetted on the white man's folly? In the West a man lives by mistakes; in the East he dies by them. And Swithinbanks knew, with mounting uneasiness, that the telegram heralded fresh trouble.

The Burmese servant, Po Shwe, a short, powerful man, stood near the door impassively, with arms folded. He knew his master wanted to speak, and so he waited, disguising a watchful alertness under an overt concern for the smooth execution of his duties. Between the two men existed a peculiar bond, above all consideration of race and social station, but observant of those basic differences.

Without looking up Swithinbanks spoke abruptly.

"There was trouble at the Arakan Pagoda today."

"I have heard, *thakin*. It is but another secret for the great turtles to hide in the sacred tank."

After twenty years in the East, Swithinbanks was not surprised at the uncanny speed with which events became known among these natives. It was as though news was bruited on some secret vibration, some alien wavelength of intuition, corresponding to the "talking drums" of Africa.

"Five *hpongyis* (priests) from the Big Pagoda are under arrest. There will be a fine and imprisonment."

"To what end, *thakin*? Idle measures—for the yellow-robed ones keep silent tongues. Only their pagoda bells speak to the winds forever and ever."

"But why was Prendergast *thakin* attacked?"

"The hill-gods are strong," the Burman said simply.

It's coming, Swithinbanks said to himself. Aloud: "Hill-gods? You speak in riddles... Listen. At the inquiry the head *hpongyi* likewise spoke in riddles. 'Beware of the death that flutters by twilight,' he said. Strange words. Now what—"

The stocky Burman went rigid. A pallor overspread his face. He stared at his master in superstitious terror.

Swithinbanks knew the courage of the man. Now, watching him, he realized as never before that the minds of these people moved in a strange region. Their very blood seemed keyed to an alien pulse; their souls diapered with the curious patterns of dark beliefs.

The Burman leaned close and spoke rapidly. "Py-a-ah! (God in heaven!) The *thakin* is favored—else the head *hpongyi* would have kept silent. You will be safe—if you keep your hand lifted."

"Me? Safe? From what?...Your words are clothed in darkness."

"But the deeds of the hill men may be even darker. Listen. The two Americans who dined here two moons ago—they have meddled with forbidden things in the hills. The flower they sought...It is true. There grows such a flower, strange and marvelous, called by the hill people the Black Flower. All meddlers who anger the priests who tend it meet death in some terrible, secret manner. More I know not. I have heard the breath of weird happenings. Be warned, *thakin*! For the gods of the hills are strong, and before them men are but *padi*-husks upon the grindstone."

Swithinbanks gazed thoughtfully through the window. His ear caught only the habitual pushing and whining in the dense bamboo clump in the compound. He could discern vague masses of tamarind trees looming immense, spectral again the distant glow of the city. Within the walls of Fort Dufferin, more than a mile square, he heard the call of a night-jar, with its curious rush of staccato notes.

The Commissioner glanced at his watch, rose and picked up the telegram. "Po Shwe, the two Americans will be here soon. *And with them comes the Black Flower!*" His tone was soft, his smile grim.

The Burman shivered as fear clutched him again. He had heard death in that soft modulation before. And surely death came with the flower. Which would reach out first?

"Should there be evil palaver with your hill-gods *tonight, *this* will do straight talking." Swithinbanks tapped his heavy automatic. "In the meantime..."

He stopped abruptly. From down the road came a sudden babble of shouting. A single shot cut through it, followed by a wild galloping, as of a horse gripped by panic, and the grind of carriage wheels.

The two men moved quickly now, snapped off the lights, and reached the dark veranda in time to see a *gharri* with one dim lamp swerve off the road, narrowly miss one gate post, and draw up before the bungalow amid a burst of oaths directed at the frightened pony by an equally frightened Hindu driver. The veranda light went on and Po Shwe was at the animal's head. Swithinbanks noted in a glance that the other carriage lamp was smashed.

Out of the vehicle tumbled two men, one tall, of commanding stature, and other short and stubby—Professor Stanton and Cyrus P. Hottinger. Had he not been aware of the gravity of the situation, Swithinbanks would have laughed aloud. Caked with mud, stained and torn, unshaven, they stood, mute evidence to the jungle's miasmic embrace, to the fierce vitality of its savage caresses.

"Hey, Commissioner!" Hottinger beamed, as Swithinbanks greeted them briefly. "Nice little reception committee." He pointed ruefully toward the road. "After we hurried back to say it with flowers, too."

Swithinbanks all at once seethed with irritation. "Do you realize…" But he got no further. Po Shwe yelled. Something flashed between him and the stubby American and crashed against the *gharri*. The handle of a great Burmese *dah,* launched with enormous force, quivered in the side of the vehicle.

"Inside!" Swithinbanks shouted as he emptied his automatic into the darkness.

And when the four men stood together again in the bolted and shuttered living room, by tacit consent their eyes sought the two large specimen cases at Stanton's feet. To Swithinbanks it seemed as though they had deferred to another Presence among them, a Presence at one hooded with mystery, leashed with threat. The Burman stood apart, bowed, staring in fascinated terror at the cases, as if they might open any moment and envelop all in the horror of some frightful emergence.

It grew on Swithinbanks that he had been jockeyed into an absurdity. He burned with annoyance, not lessened by the bland smile on Stanton's face.

"The great god Buddha has jealous gardeners. And I'm afraid, Commissioner, that they do not feel honored in the breach."

"Gentlemen, this is no jesting affair. Blood has been the price of this expedition."

"A currency," Stanton interposed softly, "that has always been minted on the dark frontiers of knowledge."

Bluntly Swithinbanks outlined the events preceding their coming. "You're in the heart of Mandalay, in Fort Dufferin, but still in the shadow of Thisbaw's Palace. You're not yet done with the priests. You've raised not a mere ripple, as you seem to think, but a major outbreak. This bungalow is probably surrounded—and death is out there, gentlemen, death!"

Stanton, listening quizzically, now bowed with mock gallantry. "Morituri…" he murmured.

In spite of himself, Swithinbanks felt a moment's admiration for the big man's serene nonchalance. But such foolhardiness seemed to take his own official responsibility too lightly.

"Very well," he snapped, "you will at once give me a detailed report of your doings. Meanwhile…" He strode to his desk and dialed headquarters. A few police round the house would rout these knife-throwing thugs.

The Americans found a closet and carefully locked up their things. One squat specimen case Stanton placed near the chair in which he sat down. They jumped as the telephone crashed and Swithinbanks wheeled.

"Line's cut!"

He sprang across the room and touched a button. A hidden niche flew open. He snatched the receiver of his private wire, exulting that he had this trick up his sleeve. He'd show these bounders outside!

Silence. For the second time he held the end of a dead line. An ice trickle of sensation coursed down his spine. As he again faced the Americans, he drew his Webley, snapped out the empty shells and carefully reloaded. Po Shwe entered quietly with drinks.

The Commissioner sat at his desk, scribbled a note and handed it to his servant. With a nod, the man glided out.

"The whole apostolic order of the yellow robe have you two spotted," he told his guests. "Po Shwe may get through. If not…" He shrugged. "Your black flower, gentlemen, may go back to the hills. And you—we…"

"'Out of this nettle, danger, we pluck this flower…'" Stanton quoted softly, smiling as he leaned to tap the specimen case.

"Since you are still pleased to joke," Swithinbanks began curtly, then changed his mind. "While we wait—your report."

Professor Stanton lit his pipe and began. Hottinger sipped his drink, blinking through horn-rimmed glasses, like a stubble-faced owl that has somehow learned the trick of humor.

Swithinbanks' attention was divided. He kept listening for the police. He felt jumpy, and, as Commissioner of Police, acutely ridiculous. Trapped and besieged in his own bungalow with all communications out! The arrogant stupidity of these Americans blithely flouting the unwritten codes of the East! The affair would certainly jam the bumbling machinery of official justice for a season. And all this mess for a confounded flower!

Thus he only half heard the tale of how these two, with three ponies and two natives guides, had left Lashio and by devious trails headed into the press of mountains for the remote village of Byat-zin; of their escape from the sucking lips of a morass where myriads of leeches had swarmed up them, stampeding the ponies; of the desertion of their guides within sight of their destination; of how native hostility turned to ready friendship when they cured the *sabwa's* (headman's) wife of an attack of acute indigestion.

Detailed, vivid, the tale unrolled. Outside an owl hooted. Swithinbanks, in a fever of impatience with this rigmarole, stiffened, listened intently. Was that a signal? Minutes went by. He heard only snatches of how they had set up a sort of jungle dispensary for the sick; of how outlying villages had sent deputations to view the white men who worked miracles; of how the feathered thickets of bamboo, of teak and pinkado, had rung with shouts and laughter as some swarthy Babe

Ruth finished a home run with a perfect slide to base in that savage stadium of the hills.

Hottinger, twinkling behind owlish glasses, chuckled joyously and slapped his knee. "The Hill Giants versus the Mandalay Panthers! Ha-ha-ha!"

The Commissioner regarded his guests coldly, jarred by their mirth. He felt they were pulling his leg. But Stanton went on smoothly recounting how they finally located the Black Flower in a tank abutting on the central pagoda and entrenched behind high palisades. They were not permitted to approach. The priests, though friendly, were firm.

And then one day a native had been dragged, wailing in terror, through the village. Stanton, curious as to his crime, had questioned the *hpongyis*. "He has offended against the sacred flower," they said. e goes to meet the death that flutters by

"He goes to meet the death that flutters by twilight."

Swithinbanks's attention suddenly narrowed to a focus. "What!" he gasped. "What was that?"

Stanton looked at him with sharp interest and drew deeply on his pipe. "Easy, Chief…Funny thing, I haven't yet figured out that cryptic saying. That night in our hut we heard that poor devil scream and gabble for an hour. One thing certain, he was inside that enclosure. And those priests shut their faces and refused to open up. We made our plans then, and one night—a festival night—we picketed our ponies in the jungle behind the pagoda. It was easy. These natives stay put after dark. *Nats*—spooks.

"At last, just before three in the morning, I stood under a great jack fruit tree that overlooked the tank. I had a short ladder and a specimen case. Our old informer in Rangoon had advised us to tackle the job *after three o'clock*. Danger otherwise, he said.

"I started up the jack tree. The night was like pitch. I didn't expect to see a thing; just stalling, sort of, till after three. About twenty feet up my foot slipped. I grabbed wildly at—anything. My hands caught a huge jack fruit on the main trunk. I recovered just as the spiked thing twisted off and fell—twenty-five pounds of solid fruit. It smacked down with a thud that shook the tree. A dog barked. I clung trembling, scarcely breathing. Slowly then, I went up higher…And all at once I had a clear view of the tank. I've been in queer places and seen some pretty queer things, but that tank topped them all."

His eyes glinted as he refilled his pipe. Swithinbanks leaned forward expectantly. A thought struck. His laugh was incredulous.

"My dear sir!...A *black* flower on a *dark* night?"

"I expected that, Commissioner. Exactly. And dark—as Erebus! A point made by the old chap had slipped my mind till then: that each flower 'had a lamp.' I tell you I *saw* those flowers. In the darkness down there floated dozens of pale, spectral moons—weird, unreal. And a heavy waft of scent came up from those marvelous blooms."

He sat up, speaking quickly.

"Another thing. Something damned curious was going on in that pond. Those flowers kept winking out, then reappearing, likely neon signs. I strained my eyes at those luminous discs—discs, mind you, more than a foot across—but I couldn't make it out. Off—on, off—on, they went. Simply fantastic! I have had this specimen for over a week and I still don't know what caused them to 'wink.'

"And staring down, I all at once remembered that a man had died there in the extremity of terror. But how? Balanced in a fork of the tree with the heavy, sweet scent from those flowers mounting in waves about me, I tried to figure it out. I felt tense and chills, and slowly a dark suffusion of horror drenched my mind. I became convinced that the Black Flower was a killer!"

He stopped, shaken even in retrospect. Swithinbanks watched him in somber speculation. For here lay the clue to the head *hpongyi's* meaning. And the solution?

"I confess to a moment of blind panic. I was ready to bolt, empty-handed. And when one of the ponies with C.P. neighed, it came as a relief. I swarmed down and crept up to the fence with my ladder. Once inside, I received a serious shock. Luminous, immense, those flowers lay at my feet—steady, <u>unwinking</u>! Simply looking, as it were. A fresh panic gripped me. Had I just dreamed them otherwise? I looked about quickly. Nothing. Only silence. Then I whipped out my knife, dropped on my knees and went to work. God! Have you heard an elephant wallowing? Ten of the huge brutes might have been gamboling there, the uproar I made. Frightened! I slashed at those tough trailing stems as though they were a matted huddle of serpents! And they fell back with the splash of severed hawsers! I pictured the whole village pouring out to investigate that rifling of their sacred tank. Somehow I scaled the fence again and hurried, stumbling, to the ponies, disposed of my precious loot in the cases and hit the back trail at once.

"By six o'clock about fifteen miles had dropped behind. Then, as we topped a rise, we heard shouting. A priest, yellow robe flying on the wind, led a posse down the trail. There was nothing for it but to drop him."

"Ah!" Swithinbanks exclaimed.

"Funny thing, Commissioner, we were left alone after that. And they could have had us a dozen times."

"Simply nipped in ahead of you, as we know. To prime the local orders."

"Sorry to put you out like this. We'll go tomorrow."

"If not before," retorted Swithinbanks meaningly, rising.

"One moment, Commissioner." Stanton snapped open the case and stood up. "You are the third white man to behold—the Black Flower!"

Swithinbanks leaned over intently. A thick, strangely sweet odor enveloped him and stole through the room. The great fleshy petals lay outspread in a kind of trembling sentience, seeming to hint of diabolical powers. But the flower's most striking quality, bizarre and startling, was its hue—a rich glossy black, like satin. He took a quick breath, fascinated, oddly disturbed. A bloom of the Night indeed, sinister, mysterious, obscene! Here was an organism he thought, which betrayed Nature in a moment of unmuzzled evil and whose rightful abode lay plunged in the darkest haunts of the jungle. He was shaken by an impulse to destroy the cursed thing, to stamp it out of existence utterly.

At a sign, Hottinger switched off the lights.

"There!" The scientist was having his hour of triumph.

And now the exotic flower seemed to put on a new proportion, to expand, to blossom with an unearthly light. It glowed, floated in the dark void like a great unwinking orb without a pupil. Swithinbanks was all at once hot, suffocated. He poured with sweat. He had had enough...Outside an owl hooted, unnoticed.

"All right, C.P."

Several clicks. "Hello," the surprised voice said, "gone haywire, I guess."

Somewhere a door opened. There came a rush of naked feet across the floor, and then a hideous nightmare burst upon the three waiting men in that shuttered room.

Things happened with incredible speed. Hottinger's voice, quenched in a heavy fall. Before Swithinbanks could snatch his automatic he received a push that spun him against the nearest wall with terrific impact. At the same moment something catapulted into Stanton, who spread-eagled over the heavy library table with an appalling crash. As they blundered to their feet, Swithinbanks drew his gun. They heard the door of the room bang, and a bolt shot into place. And now all was quiet again.

"The flower!" Stanton cried out.

"Flower be damned!" Swithinbanks said savagely. "Light—that's what we need."

A match flared briefly in Stanton's fingers and Swithinbanks found his bearings. There was a flashlight in his desk.

"You two, stay where you are," he ordered. A light touch came on his gun-hand. He drew back, halted. Almost at once Stanton spoke.

"Who touched me? That you, Commissioner? C.P.?"

Before he could answer, Swithinbanks felt something cling to his forehead. With a cry of loathing he struck at the thing with all his force. The Webley exploded and flew from his hand. A crash of glass announced the heavy slug's random mark. He held himself tense and ready, tingling all over with a nameless revulsion. Then it jumped across his mind like a flame: "The death that flutters by twilight!" My god! So this…

"Don't let the damned things settle on you!" he screamed. "The air is thick with them!"

In that locked room a grotesque battle was fought out with a silent horror that struck again and again from the shrouding darkness. Swithinbanks gave his mind to the task as to the execution of a monstrous ritual—a ritual borne of the Night, cradled in evil and forced upon him with gaunt cunning. In great gasps he breathed in the heavy, sweet air. His brain fumed as with the stealthy invasion of a drug, heralding the soft smother of catalepsy. No weakness now, he told himself; he must fight these Things until they were all blotted out. A fluttering would come, then a dreadful clinging and settling, and he would smash the loathsome thing in a sickening fury before it did its deadly work. He felt as though the Powers of All Evil were pent in that room closed in upon him…When would this end"

And when there came a cessation, barely four minutes had passed.

"That's over, thank god!" came Stanton's voice. "How about you two?"

"I'm all right," Swithinbanks managed, unsteadily.

"Cyrus!" Stanton's voice was sharpened with anxiety.

When Swithinbanks shortly probed the room with his flashlight, it picked out the dreadfully still figure of the stubby American in a corner. His face, upturned, was invisible, for it was completely covered by two giant moths. Their wings fanned gently, studded with curious whorls of color that came and went like so many peering eyes.

For a moment the two men stood transfixed, horrified. Then Stanton flung himself upon the poisonous creatures, swept them, crumpled and flapping, from his friend's face. He next dashed to the closet for his medicine chest.

"Wonderful stuff, permanganate," he said later when the little man sat up rubbing his head where it struck in the fall that had knocked him out. Two dark wheals stood out on his face.

When the lights came on—the main switch having been thrown—Po Shwe was found bound and gagged in an outhouse.

"*Thakin*, the night was full of owl's eyes."

"Never mind. The hill-gods have claimed their flower."

Swithinbanks entered that littered room in time to see Stanton step quickly to a curtained window. Deftly he imprisoned a huge moth. The other three crowded round and watched those enormous wings helplessly beating the air.

"Lord—what a fuselage!" exclaimed Hottinger.

"Gentlemen, the riddle is solved," the big scientist said. "Behold the guardian spirit of the Black Flower! For some reason they hover over the flowers till three in the morning, which explains the 'winking'—then they quit."

"At any rate, Professor, you win the consolation prize," Swithinbanks remarked drily.

The scientist smile blandly. He liked this Englishman, and he was pleased to allow him a moment's sense of patronage.

"No, no, my dear Commissioner, it's our move again. Checkmate! In that closet I have a perfect specimen of the Black Flower!"

A Test of Nerves

(This was originally published in *Month's Best*, April, 1946, the University of Washington's creative writing magazine)

Nothing could have been more lulling and serenely peaceful than that warm August evening in Southern California. I had just returned from a prescribed rest at Big Bear Lake—nerves, overwork—to find my friend, Dick Tresham, himself just back from a six-months' prowl about Mexico. From the moment of his handshake—its enormous strength almost made me cry out—I knew he had something urgent to tell me.

Our friendship was one of contrasts. While my beat was the college classroom, Dick Tresham's was everywhere. Tall, sinewy, apparently ageless, with dark brooding eyes in a face that seemed chiseled from polished bronze, he shoved around the world, keeping mostly to curious by-paths. He was a mine of odd information and strange experiences.

At nine o'clock that evening we changed into pajamas, and, with bare feet thrust out on the rug, we settled down to chat and smoke. The front door and windows stood wide open to catch the least breath that stirred. A floor lamp glowed softly, leaving the remoter corners of the room in shadow.

For nearly an hour we touched on commonplaces. I knew a story was coming, but Tresham had his own unique way of approach. He would begin with a series of ironic asides, with a curious trick of bringing a long train of thought to a sudden focus in a proverb. Then he would hold you spellbound, caught up on a vivid rush of narrative spiced with wry commentary. You alternately doubled up with laughter or sat tense, scarcely breathing.

At last, after a silence, Tresham selected another cigarette. "I've got a story for you, old man," he said slowly, "an odd story. Mexico City, like Pandora's box, lifts the lid on some queer things. Yes, queer," he repeated, "damned queer." Here he stopped and appeared to be pondering something deeply. "Women," he began again, obliquely, and with a note of irony. "There is a saying in the Punjab: 'A butting ox is better than a lonely bed.' But there is another I like a trifle better: 'One 'No' averts seventy evils.'"

A match flared and he touched his cigarette. Still holding the burning match he looked toward me meditatively. I returned his gaze, waiting. I observed that his whole attitude now became intent—sharpened, as it were. The charred fragment of match went out as it fell from his fingers. It was clear that Tresham was all at once gripped by some excitement. Knowing him pretty well, I simply assumed he was setting the stage in his own way for one of his best stories.

"Before I spin you this yarn," he said evenly (guardedly, I thought), "I'm going to check up on your nerves, give you a little test. Tried it myself—once. Now just 'freeze' for ten minutes. Only winking allowed." His smile struck me as distinctly forced. However, I smiled back and was about to arrange myself more comfortably.

"No!" His voice remained soft, but strangely edged. His eyes blazed at me with a kind of mesmeric intensity. He glanced at the clock on the mantel and nodded slightly. The test had begun. I gave in and sat motionless. An attempt to relax failed miserably.

Several moments went by like this. A frozen comedy, I thought, lazily looking across at Tresham. Looking at him, obscurely, I began to sense something curious, something measured in his fixed regard of me. Then all at once my mind closed upon an impression like a fist. *I became certain that Tresham had with difficulty held back a wild impulse to throw himself upon me!* If so, then…An unpleasant sensation coursed through me.

Straight before me the curtains of the wide front window hung motionless. I shifted my eyes to the open doorway and listened to the soft stridulation of insects on the night air. Somewhere nearby a cricket emitted a thin needle of sound. Inside the bungalow only the clock measured the silence. It occurred to me that the clock, ticking away so steadily, was one of the most arbitrary devices invented by man for measuring his little earthly concerns. For a moment I thought of the first German clock makers, then slid back to the present with a jerk.

Ten minutes:…Amusing for Tresham, yes, but what the devil did he mean…? Why, here I had been resting my nerves for a month, having tested them enough with strain and overwork. As to that it was laughable, for had I not sat in this very chair for hours oblivious to the passage of time? And now in less than ten minutes I was cramped, uncomfortable and stiff all over. A confoundedly insecure world, I reflected. Here I again looked at Tresham. His appearance almost made me sit up forward in my chair with shock.

Perspiration stood beaded on his face—not from heat, for it was cooler now. He sat there under some tremendous strain, the cause of which I failed to see. And his cigarette, smoldering unsmoked, was nearly burning his fingers. The ash lay on the rug and even as I looked he let the stub fall. It sent up a thin spout of smoke, burning a spot in the thick fabric.

This was going too far!. Test or no test I felt I must burst out with something, jump up and shake Tresham. But what—what was the matter? Something was very wrong here. For an unknown reason the room seemed to be held in a strange tension, as though an event, bizarre and unnatural, were about to be unmuzzled. Yet I could *see* nothing unusual. It was preposterous! I couldn't endure this absurd farce much longer. The whole environment appeared suddenly distorted, angular. I was terrified; at what I knew not. My nerves were at snapping point! And good heavens, why wouldn't the man speak!

Swiftly now my companion's eyes sought the clock and then came back to me. Somehow I managed to sit still, to rivet my attention on him, gaining a shred of repose from his very immobility. Confusedly I sensed a force in this man I had not suspected before. Very slowly now he spread the fingers of one hand and three fingers of the other. Eight minutes! Two more to go! But why that stealthy gesture, as though he strove to avoid being noticed? His hands trembled as with an ague.

In the split second before I thought to spring up and put an end to this scene, with the tail of my eye I caught something moving, moving. Out from the shadow cast by my chair—from under my very knees!—it glided, emerging into the light, going quite gradually, flowing smoothly across the rug like a black jet of oil—a huge rattlesnake! With petrifying terror I stared at the horrible creature. I felt a powerful impulse to draw up my feet at all costs. But once again Tresham's voice cut in warningly.

"Not a move!" he whispered tensely, moving his hand. Slight as was the movement the reptile stopped, hesitating. Then it coiled in readiness to strike. As it bunched itself together sinuously the ugly blunt head turned toward me in a baleful, sinister regard. Full in the pool of light it lay, the head flattened on the coils, tongue flickering out every few seconds. It waited, turned its head toward Tresham, appearing to gauge us, as if weighing the changes of further danger. Lying there it resembled a heavy metal spring resting on the rug.

Then I made a mistake. I saw the rattler move, thought it was making for me, and drew up my feet in one convulsive movement. In a flash the spring became a glittering rod of steel as the reptile thrust itself at me full length. A part of the body brushed one foot as the creature dropped back to the floor with the sound of falling rope. I didn't—couldn't—move. Tresham told me later that I managed a fairly creditable scream. As it was I remained engulfed by abysmal fear.

But now the spell that had held Tresham snapped. In a single lunge of incredible speed he left his chair and seized the reptile behind the head in a strong grip. Instantly the body wrapped round his arm tightly as the thing strove madly to retract its head. The dark shining coils strained and twisted, the eyes glittered dangerously while the brute's lethal mouth kept opening and shutting.

Tresham seemed to be quite at his ease now, even amused, as he held out that instrument of quick death writhing on his outstretched arm. I sat in my chair numb with fear watching this drama. I wondered vaguely what Tresham would do now with that glistening horror tight on his arm. Dimly I realized what a narrow escape I had had.

"No need to worry now," he said cheerfully. "Safe as houses this way, and incidentally as fine a specimen as I've seen anywhere."

In spite of my fear, I had to admire this man's cool nerve. Carefully now he gripped the rattler with his left hand a couple of inches below the other. Putting forth his great strength he gave a peculiar twist and a jerk. In less than a minute the coils, relaxed, fell limp.

"Handy trick," he said. "Learned that from an old Indian. Saves making a mess." He laid it out on the rug and spanned the length roughly with his hand. "A little over five feet." He rose and took the huge reptile out of the room.

I was still trembling as I stood up and looked round the place before closing the front door.

"Sit down, old man," said Tresham coming in. He took his chair once more and lighted a cigarette. I noticed his hand was quite steady. "Tell me, since when have to taken to incubating those ugly brutes under your chairs?

I gave him a sickly grin. "My nerves," I said, "they're..."

"Huh, nerves! I'm not a medico, but after tonight I'll go bail for them any time. And they came in pretty handy as an excuse. It was also lucky for you that this is the season when that dead hombre couldn't show off his rattling ability."

The burnt hole in the rug caught his attention and he bent down ruefully and touched it. "The orientals have a saying: 'The wise man sits on the hole in his carpet.'"

We both laughed at that.

Otto

Blind, and with a mind upon whose light had descended forever the pall of darkness, Otto, come out of the North, was found on the wind-ribbed strand of Gringarth. With death upon his hands he came; for around him, strewn like carrion, and with bodies angular in the distortion of splinted bones, lay three men who had essayed to stay him.

But no man knew when he came; nought found they but the one flaming word "Otto", written in letters of blood across his jerkin. Yet, just as the mind peoples the shadows with all manner of lurking monsters, so came rumor stealing to the ears of the people of Gringarth with whispers, strange and hideous, of Otto the giant, Otto the demon, Otto the devil whose strength was equal to the strength of four stout men. Seven men of the Guard had it taken to clang the mighty doors of the Black Prison of Gringarth upon him.

And there upon a certain night he lay, mute as the eternal certainty of enshrouding silence.

A spear's length without the great gate of the Black Prison paced Thorgir on his midnight post. Quickly he stepped, nervous, apprehensive, listening. Overhead the moon, pale as a silver shield, rode dimly behind the racing clouds, drenched—drenched with Death. At a slight rustle and step Thorgir pivoted like lightning, spear aloft and trembling for the swift release.

"Nay, peace, brother Thorgir, put up thy spear. It is only I."

"In truth, friend Erik, thou didst frighten me sorely. But welcome, for terrible and lonely is this vigil tonight. Nought stirs, yet I cringe before my own shadow…and the very Night is shod to escape this white desolation of moonlit sand. Silent as the Mighty Tombs of Gringarth is *he* this night."

"What! Thou speakest strangely, brother."

Overhead the moon sliced its way through billowed continents of cloud and then plunged into the clear black of the empty heavens, and the huddled, groping shadows crept out of the fair moon's far-seeing eye.

"Hast no moan, no sound escaped the devil this night?"

"Nought. Six whole hours have I paced this beat, yet no whisper hath come over yon spiked rampart. 'Tis passing strange. All seems not right within. Every night, as thou knowest…"

"Perchance the wolf doth sleep for once, friend Thorgir."

"Nay, Erik; I tell thee the wolf hath ever his day by night. Something is greatly amiss within, or else…"

"Wait—knowest thou that no morsel ate he today that I took him… And brother, 'tis very strange," and Erik's voice was but as a breath of chilling wind, "brother, the monster gazed long upon me, so long that I shuddered and cringed beneath the cold stone of his stare… Bah! His sightless eyes are terrible and ghastly to behold!"

The voices now ceased, and, graven into the immobility of silence, and with shadows like sudden black pits at their feet, the two guards merged with the brooking loneliness of the place. Then all at once, as though in very answer to their dumb expectancy, there came a fearful cry through the dim curtain of mist, knifing its white palpability which hung like a shroud about the treacheries of Death Marsh. Shrill and piercing, the cry trembled out upon the night as though torn from the throat of some luckless being trapped in the black insistence of bottomless ooze.

Mute, with the Night looking on, the two guards stood horrified, with nerves poised upon the eternity of moments. Then, like awaking dreams, they faced each other. Both their minds, by silent consent, were fixed in a single purpose.

The two figures now became detached. They crept up to the great gate that gave into the courtyard of the Black Prison, shot back the enormous bolts, and looking more like giant insects than men they hunched across the naked flags towards the far corner. Crouching low in the gloom of the ramparts they drew closer and closer, until but a spear's length sundered them from the den of Otto.

"Seest thou aught, Erik? The words crept like lost thoughts into the other's understanding.

"Hush, brother…look!"

And now in the palpable darkness appeared a form, blacker than night itself, that groped and hulked against the bars, writhing as though gripped in the strangulated agonies of the damned, momentarily visioned into the dread reality of sable flames.

To the terrified eyes of the two watchers, **it was as if the night had come alive!**

There was the suspense of a frightful moment, and then, shattering the tomb of night with their rending, two rusty iron bars were bent up like frail wires, and once again Otto was unmuzzled, vomited into existence like a monstrous birth of obscenity incarnate, gigantic in the crisis of early dawn. With the sickening agility of a new-born assurance, the being called Otto slithered across the court swiftly and hurled himself through the gates that were standing ajar. The spider-vulgarity of the thing struck the two guards into a palsy of horror. Powerless to prevent the prisoner, they crouched down and watched him disappear.

Then two horns screamed the escape to the slumbering people of Gringarth. And soon Erik, Thorgir and three men of the Guard were swift on the trail of the demon. But in a short space they all pulled up suddenly, gazing intently along the clearly defined trail and then looked into one another's faces with a grim significance, each holding the same thought.

"Death Marsh!"

Falteringly now they defiled away once more across the sands, but each knew well that no man who had ever gone into the treacherous quagmire ahead had been seen again. To both Erik and Thorgir came the remembrance of the awful cry that had wailed its own ghastly requiem.

"See," said one of the men, pointing, "the moon is pallid in the white terror of her own death!"

At last the two guards stood on the edge of the green fen. They were alone, for the three others, with hearts in the clutch of a great fear, had turned and sped back saying that the quest was nought but a useless madness.

In the dim light miasmic vapors puffed up from the swamp and herded heavily across the fetid surface, laden with the stench of black rottenness. Stooping double to follow the tracks of their quarry the two men started warily along the emerald treacheries of the only possible path that wound toward the very heart of the swamp. On either hand coiled the sluggish ooze, broken with clumps of reeds. Here and there a gaunt and sodden stump pointed like a dead and broken finger at the dismal sky. Grey lips sucked hungrily at the very feet of their imminent prey, and through the white veil from every side came the monotonous sibilance of a strange, uncanny whispering.

At length the two pursuers were compelled to stop for awhile. They stood together, silent and listening. Loose and chill, the vapor wrapped its foul mantle about them, clinging with a soft and palpable caress.

"Erik, it is as though some footless Thing were creeping in upon us!"

"Graves are but the charted havens of our days!"

Slowly now and with great peril to himself, Erik moved forward ten paces. The tracks had suddenly disappeared. No imprint could be seen anywhere. But even as they searched, puzzled, there came a muffled cry and Otto, looking immense and dim in the mist, crashed from a dense thicket of reeds. And there, in the choked silences of Death Marsh, trembling upon the slippery brink of abysmal slime, was enacted a deed such as may never be belched from the portals of hell itself. For, facing each other, each in the same moment beheld the other writhing in the dread agony of a terrible union of flesh and spirit!

Long did they stand and look upon each other, a great horror gleaming from their eyes. Then in silence they wound their way back to the safety of firm ground.

And while they stood gazing at the black towers of Gringarth, splintered against the eastern sky, they heard from far across the marshes the lost wail of a bittern… And suddenly there sped a great run of light across the hills.

The Wager

Earl Stanby—of late known to his intimates as "Duke"—and Jack Drake, the dramatic critic, lighted cigarettes and leaned back. Though they were friends, a close observer might have sensed the tension that underlay their banter.

"What! It's next week, isn't it, that…?"

"Wrong, Jack. Less than two days left. Forgotten, eh? Well, let's have a complete rundown on the deal: Situation: One Rhona Osman, star actress on Broadway, is equally in love with one Jack Drake, dramatic critic, and one Earl Stanby, former actor turned playboy. The girl can't decide which man she'll have, right?

"That's her story. Since all the principals are well heeled, money is of no account. Hence, her decision must rest on superior manly merits. Problem: She must be duped into choosing one of the handsome suitors by Monday midnight. Terms: Winner of girl compensates loser with check for five hundred. Is that clear?"

"As a summer day." The critic tilted his chair and deftly interlaced two smoke rings. He waved a hand. "Screwiest deal I ever heard of. Just a wild-cat investment in romance…"

"Duke, she's almost at the altar—with me. And…you're an odd competitor. You haven't been near her for weeks. I'm not worried. Look, in one year Rhona's jumped to top billing. She's wowed the public. And how?" He leaned forward impressively. "With this little old pen in my hand, that's how. She owes me…"

The Duke gave a deep musical laugh. "Oh, has gratitude become a love potion, Jack?"

The critic smiled tolerantly. "And what you done for her?" he pursued. "Precisely nix. You've neglected her shockingly of late. Look: for four years you take the public by storm. Why, man, they still talk of your astonishing performance in *The Double.* Then a windfall of three million drops into your lap. Pouf!...Exit actor; enter millionaire Duke. I was making a nice career for you, too, when..."

"Eternally obliged...But that's just it, Jack—prejudiced from the start. Self-advertising in the guise of criticism. Truth comes to the surface like a bubble in oil—slowly."

"Magnificent line!" The critic offered ironic appreciation. "The bubble must hurry if you're to get a squint at it by Monday."

The Duke laughed easily. The gleam in his eye held more than amusement. "Maybe you and Rhona will have a laugh on me."

"In unison, Duke! I promise to howl, to bay at the moon beneath your window." He lit another cigarette elaborately. "By the way, I've heard a lot about you lately—mostly your gilt-edged virtues." His thrust was deliberate.

"Kind fairies are scarce. Who--?"

"Rhona."

The Duke sensed challenge in the other's voice.

"Nice girl, Rhona," he said smoothly. "Twenty-two, pretty, with an alluring ripeness..."

"'Ripeness is all,'" quoted the critic, grinning.

"—and perfect architecture; witty, with something of an angel and a dash of the devil...Jack, if I didn't know you better, I'd begin looking for green in your eye."

The critic laughed boisterously. "Ridiculous!" He carefully brushed the ash from his cigarette.

"All right. Remember, the ethics of love and war are the same."

"Rough stuff, he? I'm just sh-sh-shaking with fear!...Seriously, Duke,, can you join us for the play tomorrow night? Monday night, remember. Our private theatrical ought to have a grand finale. Jimmy Hammerton will be along. Want you to meet him."

"Who's he?"

"Fellow I met about three weeks ago. Advertising game."

"Wonderful portrait. Such detail!"

"Well, he's around forty. Usually wears grey, stoops badly, has an odd birthmark over the right eye…"

"Oh—believe I've seen him. Wears glasses, and chews a mouthful of bonanza."

"That's the chap. Lord! How I detest that gilded smile and that high tenor he chirps in. But he has ideas, Duke. Quite strange ones sometimes. English, I think: distinct accent. I've brought him round a couple of times, but you were out."

"You're always scratching up enigmas, Jack. But tomorrow evening's consecrated to hamstringing two of my brokers. If you're dining later, I'll join the party."

"Better be there, Duke. This Hammerton's been sticking pretty close. He's quite a talker, and Rhona listens to him; says he 'amuses' her. Don't know what she sees in the clown, but it almost looks like a three-way competition."

"Ho, ho! The plot quickens. What's the play, Jack?"

"Ah, losing touch, Duke." The critic wagged his head. "A revival of *Lazarus Laughed*."

The Duke leapt to his feet with a sweeping gesture. "'Laugh at yourself, Caligula, if you would be master of men!'" he quoted dramatically to the startled critic. "Jack, I'll be there. I'll need some stimulation after my bloody ordeal. Like Lazarus, I must come back to life and laughter. To live greatly is to laugh greatly." He seized his hat and coat.

"At Fonelli's," the critic threw after him, "ten-thirty."

In an intimate, secluded corner, a gay little party gathered at Fonelli's the next night. Three voices fell into lively discussion. The fourth chair stood vacant.

The critic bubbled with bright enthusiasm over the play, for once impervious to Hammerton's high snorts of laughter. "The greater symbolic spectacle of the century!" he asserted for the fifth time. Between sallies he seized the menu card and scribbled notes for the next day's review. Nor was he disconcerted when Hammerton tried to pin him down to discuss the meaning of the play. "Too obvious for statement," he pronounced, and launched into an account of the Symbolic Drama.

It was past eleven when he noticed Rhona glance at her watch. "Duke must have forgotten," she said, disappointment in her voice.

The critic, jarred out of a pleasant preoccupation, flushed angrily at the reminder. "Forgotten? Huh, you're much too polite, Rhona," he said. "No, he's pointedly ignored us. Quite typical since he picked up his…"

"Mr. Drake?" The waiter handed him a note. The critic read it. His face grew dark.

"Just listen!" he spluttered. Then mockingly: "Mr. Stanby tenders apologies and says he cannot possibly be in two places at once…There you are—treats his friends like dirt. Shows his stripe! And I asked him to meet you especially, Hammerton."

"To be treated like--?" Hammerton's falsetto shrilled. "He'd be flattered at your opinion." His smile was a scintillation of gold.

"I'm going to tell you just what I think of our jingle-king. First, the man who throws up a brilliant stage career because of an accidental fortune is a fool, a lazy guttersnipe. Second, his fawning upon the Four Hundred makes him a damned social turncoat. Third, only colossal pride convinces him he's an author—after that rotten first novel. Fourth, the man who speculates in stocks and at the same time makes hair-brained wagers with his friends is a congenital idiot. And finally, any man who sets out to beat his friend's time deserves to be horsewhipped!"

While his companions sat tensely regarding him—Rhona in speechless indignation—the critic tilted back his chair and deftly interlaced several smoke rings. He close his eyes and smiled complacently. "Tonight his highness the Duke loses an important wager he made."

With a movement of incredible speed, suggesting long practice, Hammerton swept his hair over to the right. The strange birthmark, horn-rimmed glasses, mustache and gold teeth vanished into a pocket. One eye no longer drooped. His lips held an even smile as he sat erect easily.

The critic, eyes still closed and smiling dreamily to himself, heard a deep musical laugh.

"Wrong again, Jack. You go too fast. For look you, my dear Shylock..." He took a bewildered Rhona affectionately by the arm. "—my pound of flesh! Darling, you agree to marry me, don't you? Her startled gaze was melting to a warmth between tears and laughter. "It looks like bigamy," she gasped, "but you're—irresistible!"

Basements and Bargains

It all happened because my mother-in-law, an estimable lady of unflinching virtue, obeys an annual call of the blood to visit her relatives in Montana. (Be it remarkable, *sotto voce,* that this branching tribe, rooted in mountain and fen, struck from the virgin stuff of saga, appears to have sprouted in dragon-tooth fertility. The tribal tablets hints that the first freebooters came burdened with a dark freight of foreknowledge and of a promise such as pushed Jason to his frumious quest.) However ...

In a very special sense my mother-in-law is one upon whom nothing is lost: *she cannot throw anything away*—that is, not before it is scrupulously fixed. Only then is she ready to bestow her sartorial favors on those (range)-squatters whose hopes froze under the stony stare of the peaks or shriveled in the burning cauldrons of dust and desert.

For nearly a year bags, cartons, suitcases, trunks—all receive their weight of cast-offs, truculently 'saved' to await the annual day of resurrection. (The dead—O Lord!—shall indeed arise, for is there not a divinity that re-shapes their frayed ends?) Who will deny that she pushes the idiom of a priestly dogma to strange lengths, divining a useful future in all sorts of scraps and kickshaws and, like the devout Buddhist, laying all in store like so many heaven-winning virtues?

Thus for a month before her departure boxes and trunks are eviscerated. The household is convulsed with the horror of virtuous activity—creating, as my wife says, "an inter-rational incident." (I have secretly, and with much misgiving, pondered this cryptic phrase. There's a strange flux of humor in that blood!)

This year, as usual, the two ladies set up their empire in the workroom—a seething political microcosm that smacks of a private gynecocracy dedicated to the murder of moths and the absolution of the Past. The sewing machine began to cluck and chatter and hum in sudden bursts, punctuated with clicks and the dry snapping of thread. Mother and daughter, faces alight with messianic Purpose, began the magic transformations that would bring all, trimly flaunting, to the final havens of civic charity.

There came a day when I was cunningly trapped into doing furious nothings in the room. Weaving arabesques of reminiscent gossip hovered about the flying needles of reclamation.

I edged stealthily toward the door, paused. Was that a snicker behind the panel? Ah, I thought cynically, probably God and the Devil chalking their well-matched cues with Compassion and Laughter.

"Since you're doing nothing, dear," said our matriarch silkily, "you might bring up that black suitcase from the basement."

"What makes you think--!" I began violently, and stopped. Now I've never enjoyed fighting a rearguard action. I could imagine Clausewitz coldly squinting down his Teutonic nose. So I fled in headlong retreat to the basement with and 'since' snagged to my mind like a fishhook. "'Since!' Is it?" I sibilated through clenched canines, "'SINCE,' oh!" And I took a running kick at the black case. The lid flew open, and there, neatly folded, lay my own grey suit—entered service 1948, Emeritus (retired by abduction) 1951.

I stared at that well-loved suit, scarcely noticing the moth that sagged off with pendulous haste to the safer larders of a more gloomy Avernus. As I lifted the suit the great idea suddenly was born. With guilty speed I wrapped up the suit, took the suitcase upstairs and announced I would be away for the afternoon.

Two hours later, clutching my parcel tightly, I sauntered with high purpose down the streets of that section of the city where sundry dealers carry on a brisk traffic in used articles. (I have since come to suspect that in the hands of these gentry the light-fingered art of Autolycus has come to new refinement.)

The first one I went to unwrapped my parcel hopefully and held up the coat. Wordless, the man blanched at the riddled evidence. He folded it cautiously, concealing the inside, and draped the whole suit over my arm.

"Now," said the wizened homunculus, "hold like that. Go to the store on corner of next block. Find out what he give you. Then come back."

I went. The man that rose to meet me was a gigantic, bearded ruffian that looked like a ruthless myrmidon of Genghis Khan. He was less polite.

"Too much to be done," he rumbled. "Overstocked." He waved a hand at hundreds of suits hanging flattened against each other, forlornly waiting for the mean sum that would absolve their tenure. "Perhaps you'll get two dollars, not more."

I gathered my suit and returned to the first man, who bore the suggestive name of Silver. This time his tailor came over and glared at the garment savagely. He had a terrific pair of bats' ears, and I disliked him at once and without reserve. I have noted that men with such graceless appendages are afflicted with a naked allegiance to truth. This one ran true to form. He merely sniffed and walked back to his pressing machine. Silver again folded the suit.

"You take this to Mike Cohen, three and a half blocks up the street," he told me. "Ah, Cohen will prob'ly take it." He smiled, twinkled, bowed again. From somewhere behind, the tailor said, "Ah-hum,"—a hollow, throaty sound, like that heard in one of the greater cats, and not difficult to construe.

I slunk out, sensing a dark rush of atavistic impulses in which my dismayed conscience foundered. But now my purpose hardened obstinately; I became ruthless; **I would sell that suit!**—and to Cohen!

I found Mike Cohen, an undersized saurian sunning himself happily at his door. He rose and led the way to an inner room. A practiced eye appraised the suit at a glance. Next he did violent things with it, rolling it back and forth over a table in a kind of elemental indignation.

"Look, Mr. Cohen, I paid sixty dollars for that in California," I announced with historical conviction.

Cohen glared at the crumpled heap as though it had offered him a personal insult. Then, apparently addressing the garment, he hissed, "I don't care if you pay six hundred t'ousand dollars for what it was! What is it now? Not'ing!—only fit for ragpile!"

With my last shred of bluster gone, I lighted a cigarette and examined the fine points of this superb histrionic utterance. Its sheer honesty was overwhelming. I had in

vited Schacabac to a Barmecide feast! The thought suddenly restored my sense of humor, and I laughed.

"Mike, I'm sorry. I guess you're right. Throw it on the ragpile—and no feelings hurt."

That astonishing saurian crinkled his eyes, smiled widely. And all at once he dived into a capacious pocket and swiftly thrust a crumpled paper into my hand, firmly folding my fingers over it and patted the back of my closed fist. "Never mind, 's all right, 's all right," he kept saying as he now patted my shoulder and urged me gently toward the door. "Forget it. Don't tell anyone. Good-bye!" The door closed.

I never told my wife because...

You know, it's funny—but I still have strange misgivings when I think of that deal. You see, when I opened my hand, out there in the streets, I found—a ten-dollar bill! Who was the beggar?

They That Be Slain by the Sword

On a day late in March, Jean Dubé swung himself off the noon train at Grant's Crossing. He paused to watch as the express hissed, clanked and stretched again, then gathered speed and shot away down the gleaming tracks. A yellowed sheet of newspaper was snatched into the air, flapping frantically, and collapsed to the ground, where it continued hopping and spinning for a few moments in an eddy of wind—ridiculously like a chicken with its throat cut, Dubé reflected whimsically. The rapidly receding express curved into the distance, a toy train with a drifting feather of smoke.

Dubé looked around and felt amused at the solitary distinction of being the only passenger to alight here. As he pulled on his heavy coat he experienced a faint excitement at the thought of nearing the end of his journey. He felt glad that Bessie and the children had not accompanied him. No, just as well he had come alone; he would put the new place in shape for them first. He would make everything snug and comfortable, get things nicely started, and when spring arrived with warm days their new life together would commence. In its radiance the past with its mean struggles would dissolve like a dream. He would show her she had nothing to fear, that here at last was what they had been hoping for, dreaming about. He glanced toward the black press of mountains to the north. Yes, up there they would build a little paradise together.

He turned as a red-wheeled baggage truck, roughly piled with his own things, rumbled slowly across the wooden platform into the small baggage-room. The worn looking man who tugged at it almost resentfully, retained a last shred of officialdom in a shabby black cap to which hung a tarnished company badge. Two station loungers, smoking stubs of brown-paper cigarettes, sprawled on a bench beside the baggage-room door. They gawked at the stranger with unabashed curiosity as he strode up.

Dubé stopped casually before them. "Can you direct me to the nearest transfer company?"

The short of the two pushed his cap back, removed his cigarette quickly, and spat to one side.

"Ho-ho!" he roared, slapping his knee. "That's good! Er-r-Sure! The town's lousy with 'em, ain't it, Bill?" And he rocked in another spasm of mirth. The other gave a sickly grin and flicked away his wet stub.

Dubé didn't move. He stood looking quietly at them. The first man glanced up at him, and suddenly his laughter evaporated. He stood up.

"Sorry, mister," he apologized, "that was funny like." A figure came round the building at the end of the platform. "Say—there's the transfer company himself!" He chuckled, then shouted, "Hey, Pete, c'mon over, here's a break for you."

A heavy, square built, morose looking man shambled up, his hands thrust deep in the pockets of his dirty overalls. Dubé explained where he wished to go.

The old man stared hard at the speaker for a moment, then drew a rough hand across his seamed, stubbly face. With a quick twist of his head, he ejected a brown stream from his lips. His eyes moved uncertainly toward the mountains and up at the sky.

"White 'Orse? Christ! What in hell…?" He seemed to change his mind abruptly. "Huh, thirty mile clear, two thousand up. Ticklish climb mostwhiles." His face puckered with indecision. "Heavy stuff?

he asked cautiously, peering into the baggage room. He pulled out a heavy watch on a leather thong. "Well…" he began, then suddenly made up his mind. "All right, mister. Guess I'll risk it. Call me a darn fool, anyhow. Take you up for fifteen bucks."

Dubé nodded helplessly. There was no other choice. Within a few minutes, the old man's battered little truck was packed with his scanty belongings and the small settlement was dropping behind.

Though the sky was heavily overcast objects emerged with a detailed distinctness that made their actual distance a bewildering deception. The mountains, though fully twenty miles away, seemed to rush upon them and yet remain guardedly remote, jutting abruptly, massing together in tremendous conclave, jostling with headless hunching shoulders.

Steadily they approached the first sprawling foothills. Except for an occasional grunt old Pete kept stolidly silent. At length, with another prodigious grunt, he put his companion a gruff question.

"'Scuse me, mister, it bein' none o' my business, but how come you be goin' up to them Bluffs?"

"Oh, traded land in the south of Washington for the Bluffs farm up here. Looked like a good deal to me. Party by the name of Van Ness. He said…"

"Eh? Dirk—Dirk Van Ness?" There was a grim note in the old man's voice.

"Why, yes. Know him?"

Old Pete spat emphatic contempt.

"Jeeze, *do* I! Smooth blackleg, old Dirk was. Nothing' good ever come out o' him, I can tell you. Time was when I steered folks clear o' any dealin' with Dirk. Slimy bastard, that's Dirk! He lay for all the suckers…Huh, trade you, did he? Done you, most likely!"

Jean Dubé stared ahead at the road, and then regarded his companion with a faint stir of uneasiness. He had believed Van Ness. Why, he had even seen the recent pictures of the place the man had produced, together with last year's official statement of yield. Surely there couldn't be any mistake…True, he had not seen the place itself…And Bessie, of course, had been all for caution; but then Bessie always had been over-prudent, always raised objections. A man simply had to take a chance sometimes. Who didn't? It was quite probable, too, that old Peter was one of those habitual croakers to whose gloomy mind nothing and nobody seemed straight. He, Dubé, had met that kind before… Still, what if…? Dubé bent forward to view more clearly the thunderous blue-black of the mountains which now swooped close upon them. No, he dared not permit himself even to think of any alternatives—now.

"See here, mister," the old driver went on, "I'm sure sorry, I am. Too bad I couldn't have put you wise somehow. But let me tell you: come this spring, I been around these parts twenty-seven years. No plough nor team been on that Bluffs farm for eight years now. Pesky place's wild, all growed over with weeds. 'Ceptin' old Burt Nevin and his two boys—'about half-mile down the road from the Bluffs—I seen only hungry men come down off this here mountain…And some I know—never come down again."

With this cryptic addition the old man turned to the other. They looked at each other silently for several moments. Then the road curved round and began to climb steeply along the mountain side, demanding all the driver's attention and skill. Dubé felt in that silent exchange a mute admission that there was nothing more to say. As the track tilted more sharply upward all other thoughts fled from his mind. He sat tensely clinging to his side of the machine, wondering only how much farther it was to the top.

Recent rains had made the ground heavy, and the small truck spun dirt and gravel from beneath the thrusting wheels. The engine gasped and labored, seeming almost ready to give up the fight. But they crept steadily upward. The road had evidently fallen into disrepair; the once protecting bank had slid away in places, forcing them to skirt along the edge of fearful declivities with the machine often tilted at a sickening angle. Several times they stopped to remove fallen boulders and to dig away mounds of earth and rubble. Once a bare clearance was found under a mighty cedar that spanned the narrow road.

The old driver never spoke during that climb. He kept growling under his breath, and frequently ejecting a dark jet from his lips. Would the trail ever become a normal level again, Dubé thought fearfully. What a fool he had been to come up here! He studied the trail, fascinated. It hugged the mountain, slid slyly round great jutting rocks, glided straight out across the edge of dizzy escarpments, unexpectedly writhes back upon itself in a sudden black coil.

When at last they crawled out upon the upper flats Dubé felt exhausted with the long tension he had sustained. The old, little-used road now skirted along dense pine woods for several miles. They passed by the first signs of human habitation up here: a neat, white farm house set in the midst of ordered rows of leafless fruit trees. Old Pete jerked a thumb in that direction:

"Burt Nevin's," he said laconically.

Now that he was nearing the end of his journey, Dubé felt a gloomy foreboding press down upon him. The sanguine spirits in which he had set out were all but dissipated by the old driver's words. He looked out at the pines, massed closely together, standing there straight and quiet, black forms that leapt at the heavens like countless daggers. He had had no idea...This was not what he had expected. Why hadn't Bessie...no, why hadn't he, *he*, Jean Dubé himself...? And why, why..." His thoughts became vague and confused as the machine lurched into a wildly overgrown drive and slowly tore a way through the weeds, finally coming to a stop by a small farm house discolored with age.

For a few moments he made no effort to stir, only let his eyes move across the limit of his vision. So this was his land now, his home: one hundred and twenty acres he had never even looked at. Peaches and apples. Well...Paradise! Out of this wilderness?...How terribly right the old man had been!

In the meantime the driver had nearly finished bundling his things on to the narrow porch. The old man seemed to be in a great hurry. He almost snatched the bills Dubé held out to him.

"March," he said, vaguely apologetic. "Dark soon. Maybe rain tonight…Goodbye, mister, and—good luck."

The engine roared and shuddered, and he huddled down over the wheel like a huge misshapen insect, intent only on hastening away. Dubé watched the truck jolt down the long driveway until it turned into the road, and disappeared.

Complete silence closed down once more. He had a curious impression that the driver and his machine had been in strange, secret league with each other to get rid of him as though he were an unwanted, disagreeable burden.

He looked at his watch: four o'clock.

Shivering now, he drew his heavy coat closer and walked to the rear of the deserted house. He stood quite still, gazing across the acres of leafless trees, across toward the blackening west. He remained standing there a long time, stiff and unmoving, like an object deeply rooted, slowly comprehending the seeping essence emanating from the place. And gradually, with a kind of blind, unctuous advance, a dark unreasoning terror edged into his consciousness, slugged itself upon his mind.

For Jean Dubé suddenly felt trapped; trapped and betrayed to forces at once clever and cunning, devilishly cunning; forces that had decoyed him at last to their remote and desolate fastness, and were now covertly watching him with amused, ironic malice, sure of their kill, and closing in upon him with calculated stealth. He wanted to fly, to run screaming from this ill-omened spot, but he knew that retreat was not impossible, knew, like a man flung upon a desert island, that all roads of escape had become fathomless and uncharted. Something wild in him, something primitive and untamed, rocketed to escape, only to rebound from invisible bars, hurt and stunned.

"Sucker!" he exclaimed through clenched teeth. "My God! What a sucker!"

Old memories began to swoop like great cloud-shadows across his mind. His home in Canada...His father—a hard, bitter, dominant man. Life had bitten its jagged defacement upon the cold iron of his nature. His mother, gentle and affectionate, had suffered terribly under his father's exacting cruelty, and had died at last of grief and disappointment when he, Jean, was only ten. But he had always remembered her dying injunction never to let his father break him to his obstinate will. "Never be driven into anything you have no mind to do, Jean darling," she had said. Later, it was this that had made him hold out against his father's blind arbitrariness in wanting him to read for the bar. At last the old man had exploded: "Very well, you young fool, since you are so determined to choose your own way, understand that this house has never been a hang-out for shiftless idlers—and never will be! Always contrary—like your mother! (How he, Jean, had surged with sudden anger at that!) You can get out. I've done with you. And mind, no coming back here whining like a beaten cur!" He remember how, late that night, without a word of parting, he had slipped away, turning his back forever upon the house that had come to hold nothing for him but the hungry ghosts of a lost happiness. Quietly he had dropped out of the old life...

Hungry men...hungry ghosts...how they pressed upon one!

And now his mind lifted with something of its old thrill at the thought of the next four years of freedom. Summer and winter, freely had he ranged the great forests and the open wilderness, learning their secrets and conquering their terrors. He had worked over toward the Canadian Rockies and had become known as one of the most intrepid of hunters and skillful of trappers. He learned to set a trap with such self-effacing cunning and wizardry, even to removing all trace of human scent with strange mixtures smeared over his gloves and shoes, that the most wary of beasts fell easy prey to him. His name became a by-word in the country for daring prowess. At the trading stations he was looked upon with special favor, for he brought in the choicest pelts. He became that rare ting: a lone trapper with a tidy sum of money...

And now his pulse quickened at the memory of how he had once come upon Stillman's Hollow, a remote little hamlet in the north. It appeared that the scattered community had been scourged for years by a great lone wolf. Lightning Dick had become a ten-year legend. It was given out among the knowing ones that he was twice as large as the average of his species. Strange and fearful things were reputed to have happened in his wake. Children had disappeared; and men, trudging through the forest alone, had been terrified by the most appalling yodeling breaking out in nearby thickets. But never a glimpse did they get of the animal himself on such occasions. He had been seen to sweep through the woods like an evil shadow. And on bitter nights, when men kept near their fires and great trees cracked like rifle-shots, his deep-throated cry floated out over the valley like a bugle upon the startled air, at once a menace and a challenge. Even tried hunters had at last given up the pursuit in superstitious dread; it was uncanny, they argued, like trying to trap a sound, a shadow.

Dubé had listened to all their stories, and had then gone to work quietly. Secretly he laughed at the absurd notion of a wolf that could elude his practiced skill. Nevertheless, he took special pains for there to be no bungling. He would show these hunters what real trapping was! And so, with tireless patience, he essayed all the subtle, expert cunning of his craft. He laid his traps in the woods and far up the valley. The days slipped by into weeks and still they brought him only the negative success of unwanted game. Yet, curiously enough, some of his most carefully set traps were insolently sprung, and examining them with astonishment and suspicion, he felt an awe mingled with respect for so astute an adversary. Clearly marked in the snow or on the earth there appeared the print of great pads which identified the bold trespasser. After three months of futile labor he admitted to himself that here was something, a veritable intelligence, in the face of which the usual methods became so much clap-trap, mere crude artifice. And, not least among his annoyances, Dubé now sensed he had become an object of pitying amusement, if not of active resentment. The natives all at once evinced a pride in Lightning Dick outwitting the stranger.

And then there were other things. For, always aware of imminent presence with a kind of seismographic sensitivity, there were moments when, bending over his cunning deceptions, Dubé suddenly felt himself to be the isolated focus of unseen watchers, watchers that leered at him, covert and intent, great jaws slavering with impatient malice. He would whip around, fearfully expectant, only to see the silent brooding forest stretching everywhere. Yet he would finish hastily and hurry away, gripped by a nameless fear... He began to understand the hunters' tales. Queer and uncanny, he admitted reluctantly.

In vivid retrospect Dubé evoked the final scene in what had become, by a curious shifting, an intensely personal struggle, involving issues at first wholly unsuspected, irrelevant. Clearly he was opposed to a subtle force that shrewdly comprehended his bungling strategy and casually unmasked its weakness. All at once the contest assumed a kind of moral purposiveness; in some strange way, he felt, his whole future was being hammered into design in the fires of a crucial experience. He must not now admit failure; success had become an imperative necessity. Grimly determined, he sat down and took careful thought, reviewing the situation critically, probing all the likely possibilities in this bizarre game. In the end he devised a sly trick; upon it he staked all.

On a day in early spring, when a steady thaw had scabbed over the once unbroken white wilderness with bare black patches, and the streams, unleashed, flung themselves down the valley with a mad shout, Dubé set a trap such as he had never set before—a double trap, a trap within a trap. First he selected a little clearing, and then stealthily reconnoitered the surrounding country. Beyond a few birds that had come back to the valley early no other sign of life stirred. After circling about for several hours he came back to the clearing and worked fast. When he had finished he inspected the trap carefully. With satisfaction and even a touch of surprise, he noted that the spot looked entirely innocent and natural. The sharpest eye would never have suspected the presence of the two pairs of powerful steel jaws that would snap shut in a wink at the slightest movement. The larger pair could only be sprung by the smaller one inside.

Dubé next built a rough lean-to on a ridge about a mile from the clearing. Here he stationed himself and swept the valley with powerful glasses. Two whole days crept by without a sign. He looked out upon a melting world with every channel swollen with a brown flood. There was a steady roar like that of a great wind rushing fabulously through the trees and funneling up the black gorges. He felt that his last effort had failed, that he was the victim of a strange mockery.

Early on the morning of the third day, before the sun had topped the highest ridges, he awoke and lay still, staring with dull apathy at a drop of water that gathered and fell monotonously in a corner of his shelter. Somewhere near by a loosened mass of snow collapsed heavily. He reached for his glasses—for the last time, he told himself—more out of habit than from any expectation. He stood up and stepped out into the brisk air. A thin haze hung in the valley as he once more lifted the glasses and focused them on the clearing. The sun suddenly flamed from behind the eastern ridge and a long shaft of light fell across the black woods below like a sword. At the same moment he went rigid and intent, straining his eyes. Something had happened down there, but he couldn't quite get it clear. He slung the glasses, seized his rifle and went springing down the slope, over slippery boulders and great fallen trunks. In ten minutes he stood on the edge of the clearing and knew that his long vendetta was at an end.

There lay the great beast, crumpled over the trap, as though gathering something into an agonized embrace, with both forelegs caught in the cruel vise. With heaving chest and twitching flanks, lathered over with blood and dirt, it had evidently struggled for hours in a desperate fury to disengage itself, biting and tearing at the cold steel with mouth lacerated and teeth splintered. In all his varied hunting experience Dubé had never beheld such a passionate, elemental struggle for life. He stood there, deeply strangely moved, feeling guilty and penitent at having ruthlessly destroyed so magnificent a creature, crushing such beauty and wild strength into the earth like a detestable insect.

Almost at its last gasp now the huge animal moved its head and looked at him with tortured eyes. Was it mere fancy, or did Dubé catch a dull flame of reproach leaping in their somber depths? In the presence of that final agony he felt a surge of bitter humiliation come over his entire being. It was as though he had been guilty of a desecration, or had committed an irremediable crime against God and nature... Stepping forward quickly, he raised his rifle. Lightning Dick shuddered convulsively, went limp and lay still forever. Dubé then turned and fled from that tragic scene as though pursued by a phantom. Without a word he disappeared from Stillman's Hollow; but the memory of that gaunt, lonely drama had remained undimmed, bitten upon his mind to the last detail.

Standing there in that oppressive silence, Dubé shivered and drew a hand across his forehead in a vague effort to brush away such disturbing memories. The events of the following years became a confused medley: his coming down into the States; his meeting Bessie and their hasty marriage; his futile struggle with the small farm in southern Washington and his dwindling capital, with the growing expense of the children that came in steady succession—Virgie, now ten, and later Ben, Don and Jeanette, who was four...And last of all his meeting with Van Ness; and now—this. But it was no use going over that again.

Bessie... Something had happened to poor Bessie, something inside, turned her to stone. Perhaps here...here...

He returned to the present with a shock and moved forward slowly, glancing about him. A little to one side and about forty yards from the house, a dilapidated barn, once white but now stained and discolored through long exposure, squatted like a monstrous death's head, two empty square sockets brooding and staring from above, and a barred stable entrance grinning evilly below. Rains had hammered and storms learned their weight upon it until it had sagged forward. To the silent regard of the man it conveyed the odd impression of a monster that, disturbed at some horrid practice, had glanced up slyly at a sensed intrusion.

Behind this the ground rose gradually and ended where the abrupt ridge of the Bluffs swept round in a curve. Black and treeless, the splintered outline of the rocks jutted menacingly against the somber sky, looking for all the world like the iron teeth of some gigantic trap!... So he was trapped, was he? Trapped like an animal—like a wolf. Dubé went taut. By heaven!—Trapped like—like—

With such suddenness did this thought fasten upon him that Dubé burst into shrill, mirthless, laughter. Just as suddenly he broke off, appalled at the grotesque effect of his own voice in that deathly silence. Thin and distinct, a faint laugh was flung back at him from the black ridge. The sense of his utter loneliness rushed upon him; he shook in a quick surge of panic. And all at once it seemed to his distraught mind, as his eyes took in the even row upon row of dark and leafless trees stretching up the slope, that they stood there, a terrible regimentation of dead and broken hands thrust up through the earth by some swart eruptive force stirring beneath, avid to seize upon the solitary human trespasser should he venture within reach.

In the settling gloom Jean Dubé, white and haggard, turn and fled into the empty house.

Part II

The next day moved upon the mountain with a bleak insipience. The clouds, bellying low, fumed and boiled in white silence about the black lines of the Bluffs. The fine rain of the night had ceased. And when the light widened, thin and ghostly, it conveyed the curious impression of sliding into the space left by the enormous, slowly lifting pall of darkness. Gradually it invested the house, crept into the front room, unmasked objects without transfiguring them. It stole upon the sleeping man, seeming to hover dimly above him as if diffident of its own revealing intrusion; then gathered and pushed on toward the dark corners, leaning its grey empire against the last mystery of night. The sleeper sighed heavily, stirred uneasily. One arm slowly fell away from across his body and lay straight by his side, the fingers oddly clenched, challenging.

For several waking moments Dubé's mind swam smoothly in an effortless suspension devoid of thought, before the lean anguish of memory swirled down and stabbed through his consciousness. He sat up, once more intensely aware of his presence in the empty house, cut off and alone, once more faced with the grave need of measuring himself against the evil turn that had thrust him on to this bitter testing. And once more he began to feel a sharp access of fear.

He jumped up, stretched, and shook himself. "You fool," he told himself briskly, "you're getting as jumpy as a cat. Better get to work before..." He glanced round quickly, unable to control a growing uncomfortable sense of being an interloper, an intruder, where strange, secret rights, of another kin from his own crude rights of trade ownership, asserted their ancient precedence. Perhaps its long, slow retreat from the homely ties of human relationships had conferred upon this house a character at once peculiar, withdrawn, subtly dividing its movements to an alien rhythm and whispering its meanings in a sinister idiom. This disturbing impression only strengthened during the succeeding days into a kind of certainty, but a certainty that found no mechanism for proof. He would step into the door and suddenly stop, frozen with an over-mastering conviction that he had pushed in upon a soft sibilance of many voices. The very air seemed to hold a threat. A presence, sentient and watchful, seemed to pervade the place; a presence that resented his interference and claimed the privilege of native ground.

And strange personalities, unknown to him had lived there moved within these walls, hearts glutted with fear and hatred, and laughter drained of radiance. They had vanished, but something of them yet remained, detached, living, clung like an invisible wraith to the rooms and became a part of their silence. Every house, Dubé thought, retains, by some inscrutable chemistry, a vague but indelible stain of the identities it has once encompassed.

He now decided to follow his first impulse and be brusque with himself. It wouldn't do to succumb to fantastic imaginings. There was work to do, work that claimed all his energies and attention. He affected a jaunty whistle, stepped across the room and casually straightened an old text card hanging awry. It was green, with a flourish of silver lettering. But he did not read it. It occurred to him that Bessie would bring some pictures that would look well on these walls. He realized, too, that he was decidedly hungry.

After swallowing a mouthful of stale food, he looked over the house and set about cleaning it out as best he could. Clouds of dust arose as he made a heap of the rubbish and tore down the cobwebs hanging everywhere.

He began to feel better as he grew more used to his surroundings. But somewhere deep within him, Dubé was dimly aware of a pulsing and vibrating, like the trembling of a tightly strung nerve or fiber.

For a moment the physical activity of work created in him the subtle delusion of a problem successfully met, of a solution unexpectedly snatched from a world sinking into formless disaster. And because in him illusion had always been a swift fugitive from the grim reality of things, as soon as he had finished cleaning, he hurried into the coat and plunged off through the shaggy weed-choked orchard, intent on forcing himself into a familiarity with his whole property, gauging the extent of the task ahead of him. But he hardly dared to let his mind touch the fact of his terrible lack of equipment.

Once only did Dubé stop to look round at the gaunt rows of trees raying away from him on all sides. Scabbed over, rotting, hopelessly burdened with dead limbs, they seemed to stand there shivering, mutely begging for pity and forgiveness: like withered old women, palsied with neglect, ashamed, reproachful and desolate, unshriven in their last dishonor of fruitlessness. With a shudder at the strange thought, he pushed on.

Thus for two whole days he held himself to the urgency of exploring every yard of ground. Sometimes he broke savagely through the rank, tangled wilderness, slashing and hacking a way with triumphant ferocity, unconsciously finding in mere movement a substitute for lost convictions, a deceptive anodyne for tottering courage. Like a man overtaken by a blizzard, Jean Dubé moved in a world of lost directions. He knew there was no going back. He could only choose his one conditioned alternative. And so, selecting a point, he stumbled forward blindly, fearfully, without compass, sightlessly leaning into the storm.

Toward the close of the second day Dubé found himself clambering back down the precipitous sides of the Bluffs. For an hour he had sat on the bleak ridge, a dark silhouette, silently staring across the valley, watching the mists far down rise and herd together in white clumps, then slowly move, meet and merge, blotting out everything. Arrived at the foot of the rocks, he came to the dense thicket of pines and cedars that sprang up before him and defined the sweep of the buttressing Bluffs. The grove covered that corner of his land, extending in a fan for a quarter of a mile. Directly before him a narrow ravine cut through the grove, evidently forming the drainage outlet for the eastern slope of the Bluffs. It started abruptly and slid like a dark, jagged cicatrice through the trees. Dubé decided to go down this instead of skirting round.

He immediately found himself in a dim twilight through which he moved warily, picking his way over boulders, fallen logs, and great banked up knots of debris. The eerie silence that enveloped him was broken only by the sounds of his progress—the scrunch of pebbles, the snapping of driftwood, the splash of his feet through still, black pools, his own breathing as he drew in the heavy, dank air of the place. Then the ravine began to widen and became shallower. The trees opened out and he could see where the apple orchard started. Beyond rose the old barn and the roof of the farm house.

Dubé felt a distinct relief to be getting free of the gloomy thicket. With the hunter's sensitiveness at knowing himself to be the only moving object in the landscape, he stopped for a moment before leaving the belt of timber. It was then that, happening to glance between two trunks into the little glade beyond, Dubé's eyes fell upon a sight that transfixed him with horror. Under the thick brown mat of pine needles the earth swelling into three mounts, a large mound flanked by two smaller ones. And over the sagging wooden crosses that marked them crept a green leprosy of moss.

In a flash the haunting words of old Pete invaded his mind: "I seen only hungry men come back off this here mountain. *And some I know—never come down again.*" It was all clear to him now. From those three quiet graves, hidden away from curious eyes, the mute tragedy of the past seemed to swoop like a terrible revelation of the future and fasten upon him. Something pent up in him broke down, gave way in a wild flood. Scarcely knowing what he was doing, Jean Dubé fell upon his knees shaken by a storm of sobbing.

"Oh, god," he cried, "not that!...My babies! My poor little babies!"

All about him the trees stood silent, remote, darkly aloof from the spectacle of human grief. Stiffly they held out their branches, only to catch once more the thin rain that began to whisper among them. Gasping, half blind with tears, Dubé rose and ran headlong from that ill-omened spot. He had a frantic desire to hide himself away, to find some deep stillness where he would be secure from the strange forces that seemed in league to mock him, to dart their terrors upon him; from forces that existed solely to entrap him, to thrust fumbling fingers into his very soul, creeping down into inner darkness with the blind sentience of roots determined to split open the last stronghold of sanity.

In that short flight to the house one thought drummed above all others and clove through the confusion in his mind. It thundered like great hammer-blows upon his brain: "Hunger, Dubé!—They died of hunger—HUNGER!" Again and again, as though bursting from some great voice enveloping him, the terrible words swept through his consciousness. His hat was gone. His wet hair poured over his eyes in a dark flood. His eyes themselves, fixed unnaturally, stared straight ahead, making his face, now drawn and blanched with fear, all the more startling. Moving as in a dream, tormented with the supreme urgency for speed, his legs seemed turn to stone, every step clogged and dragging, every breath a murderous fog of knives.

Somehow he blundered round the corner of the barn and drew near the house. "Hunger, Dubé!" the voice screamed again, "HUNGER!" ending in a shriek of strangling laughter. Almost spent, almost ready to give up, he did not notice the figure that shouted and waved to him from the corner of the house. And suddenly, when nearly at the door of his sanctuary, he tripped and fell headlong. A terrible frenzy of anger boiled up in him as he became acutely aware of the tall, rank grass in which he lay sprawled. For years it had been stealthily marching upon the house to engulf it, leaning against it now, caressing it, hungrily licking at the weathered old boards. In a mad paroxysm, Dubé struggled up and flung himself upon the tangled mass, screaming and trampling it down, tearing up great handfuls in his strong fingers.

In puzzled astonishment, the newcomer stood regarding the unexpected and extraordinary scene before him. Then he strode forward. Dubé felt himself held by powerful arms.

"What's taken you, man?" the stranger said sharply. "Better get hold of yourself. What's happened?"

Dubé stood up shakily, feeling dazed, dimly aware of the presence of the other man. From one hand hung a knot of grass and earth. He leaned against the house, his chest heaving from his furious exertions. As he looked at the stranger his fingers slowly relaxed and the grass slid from them, A sudden faintness came over him; he grasped clumsily at the house for support.

"Easy, easy," the man said, stepping up to him. "You'll feel better in a minute."

With an effort, Dubé straightened up. Though he felt drained of all strength, his head was clearing again. He began to feel ashamed as he thought of the curious spectacle he must present. At the same time the presence of the other man communicated a glow of comfort.

"Sorry," he said, making a vague gesture in the direction from which he had come. "Thanks, anyhow. I'm better now. But who—who—?"

"Nevin—Scott Nevin." The other held out his hand. "Pop had me come over to take you back to dinner, get acquainted like. Of course, you're Dubé—old Pete told us; besides, here's a letter for you. Come on now. Wash up over home." But Dubé, hesitating, looked at him with troubled eyes. "Don't worry," Nevin added reassuringly, "I won't say a word."

Scott Nevin's car stood in the drive, and as Dubé dropped into the seat beside his companion a peace descended upon him, a sense of serene reassurance in this renewed alliance with familiar things. He gave himself over to the will of the other man, whose voice rambled on pleasantly. Dubé at silent, unlistening, his mind deliciously free from the nagging insistence of disturbing thoughts.

Soon they turned in at the other house. In a little while Dubé was standing before a cheerful fire in the living room.

"Here's our neighbor, Pop," Scott Nevin said as he brought Dubé in from the kitchen.

In a deep leather chair near the fire sat an old man. Though the eyes he now turned on the two young men were faded, they were lit with a surprising animation. In them gleamed a kind of imperishable gluttony for life. With bird-like eagerness they darted from one man to the other. A thin white stub of beard wagged incessantly on his chest as he alternately pouted his lips and then sucked them back over toothless gums. He was one of those creatures out of whom Time, in a spirit of sly self-mockery, makes a fantastic and suggestive caricature of itself: the once heroic lineaments of the man are slowly muddled into a clownish grotesquerie; every line and feature reveals the insidious corrosion of the years. The old man, huddled in his chair, was wrapped in a voluminous cloak and wore a black skull-cap. In the tricks of firelight he looked like a gigantic gnome about whose form floated a dark nimbus of the night. This strange effect was completed as the combined shadows of the man and the chair leapt and writhed upon the deep-toned paneling of the walls—now gibbous, sinister, frightful, now in a wild and soundless sarabande.

"Heh, heh!" the old man whinnied in a high falsetto. "You're real welcome, neighbor, real welcome. Heh…night two days back"—he jerked quickly toward his son—"Scott, you scallywag! You sh'd be ashamed o' yourself! Light the lamp and tell Annie to fix things nice, and like as not Dave is waitin' for help with the killin' in the yard. Hurry, 'fore it's too dark."

Scott went out, and the old man turned complainingly to his visitor. With trembling fingers he laboriously filled a black stump of a pipe. He kept shaking his head hopelessly.

"They never mind me no more now. In the old days what I said, went; but no more, no more." Shakily he held a match to the pipe, moist lips sucking desperately at the stem which they seized with clammy tenacity. For another minute he sat brooding, then his face lighted up. "Heh, heh! But I'm getting on, young man, getting on—heh!—I be nigh on eighty-five!" He chuckled and bent over his pipe, his scanty beard wagging furiously on his chest. He fairly glowed with the senile triumph of the aged at defeating their last enemy, time. He stopped suddenly and glanced up, a cunning eager look coming into his sunken face as he scanned the room hurriedly to make sure they were alone. "Sh-h-h," he cautioned mysteriously, lowering his voice and shooting out his lips, "they don't believe me when I tell 'em, but I got a funny kind o' spin in my head, a spin—and a kind o' knockin' sometimes, a gallopin'. Annie, she kind-a understands—but the boys—. Queer, queer,"—he shook his head disconsolately—"and when I tell 'em—"

The old man broke off abruptly as the door opened and Scott stepped in with a lamp in his hand. He seemed to shrink visibly while he huddled down farther in the deep chair, fumbling hurriedly with his pipe and looking as guilty as a child caught in a forbidden act. Scott set the lamp on the table and shook a reproving finger at his father.

"Ah-ha, Pop, at it again! Botherin' visitors with your 'spin'." He turned to Dubé. "Come on out back and meet Dave."

All this time Dubé had stood listening to the old man, now and then murmuring a vague response. When he now moved toward the door with Scott, he was aware that old Nevin's eyes sought his own in pathetic appeal. "You see," they seemed to say, "didn't I tell you!"

In the yard Scott called to his brother. The figure that approached was that of a man obviously younger than Scott, but taller, gaunt and angular. Without a word he held out a stiff hand to the visitor. Dubé found no visible point of resemblance between the brothers. The dark, lupine face was quiet, but not tranquil; waiting, but not expectant; and Dubé, looking at him, sensed a storm behind his eyes. A strange, unpredictable being, Dubé thought, feeling suddenly uncomfortable as he followed the two men to where a calf was hobbled and tied midway between two trees.

"Everything's ready," Dave said in a surly tone. "Been ready for the last half hour. Thought you'd never be coming. And seeing how you like this work and I don't..." He picked up a butcher knife and tested the edge with his thumb.

At the approach of the men the wretched animal seemed to know that something terrible was about to happen. In a frenzy of fear, it kept stupidly switching its tail, making frantic ineffectual lunges to break free, lowing dismally in a quickening terror.

In the falling light Scott stepped firmly up to the calf and lifted a ponderous sledge. The last despairing cry of the stricken beast broke dreadfully in its throat as the blow fell upon its head with shattering force. It shuddered and crumpled slowly upon the ground. But even before the final collapse, Dave stooped swiftly, thin lips drawn back over bared teeth, and slashed its throat in a sudden voltaic fury, and, as it seemed to Dubé, malice. Blood spouted through the vent. Once... twice...three times he drew his knife with passionate violence through the open gash, as though bent on a mad effort to sever the head clean from the trunk. All at once he stopped, rose and savagely kicked the warm trembling body at his feet. He appeared oblivious of the presence of the two witnesses, who stood fascinated, staring in thrilling horror at the demonic transformation that had risen and swept over him like a suffusion of evil. For a few moments dreadful sounds bubbled out with the pulsing gouts of blood as the calf continued to cry feebly through its severed gullet. Then it lay slack and still.

Scott Nevin and Dubé were silent and rigid spectators of this scene. To Dubé not only was it an act of inexplicable and unwarrantable savagery, but it had come unheralded, had startled like a red blade of flame leaping from a gloomy house. But the strange uprush of passion had subsided as suddenly as it had come. For Dave stared straight before him in a kind of dull abstraction, with even a tinge of wonder, like a man who hears within him a voice he has never known before. At the same time he seemed morose and withdrawn. The wet knife drooped from his hand; bright, thickening beads gathered at the point and fell at his feet in a dark spot that stealthily expanded.

In a single swift movement Scott now stepped up to his brother. His eyes blazed, his hands were clenched. "You dirty skunk!" he said slowly in a tone cold with level contempt. "If that's the way you feel—" He stopped without finishing. David looked at him then as though he had noticed his brother's presence for the first time. He seemed preoccupied with some thought.

"Funny, I...I didn't really mean..." He stammered and broke off, confused.

Scott, deeply troubled, continued to scrutinize his brother for a few moments. Then he half turned away from Dave and putting a hand on the other's shoulder, pressed it silently. His averted eyes were almost pleading as they met Dubé's. "Never mind, Dave boy," he said conciliatingly without looking round, "never mind." And all at once he was gone, hurrying away into the house.

As Dubé followed the retreating figure with his eyes he received an odd, oblique intimation that in Scott's pleading glance lay the explanation of his earlier promise of silence.

He watched the door close upon Scott. Left out there with Dave Nevin he began to feel wretchedly out of place, ignored, and uneasy.

He wanted to say something to this strange being, to tell him… His thoughts snapped abruptly as he turned and found those tormented eyes looking intently into his own. He waited for the other to speak.

"Why the hell are you up here?" Dave burst out at last, with sudden harshness. "Christ! What do *you* expect to do with the Bluffs? Don't you know what happens up there every time?" Without pausing for an answer, he went on savagely: "God! How I hate this place!" The knife swept round in a swift arc, "I hate them all, I hate every tree out there! Pegs—to hold me down!…They're all crazy, keeping me back. They don't know what they're doing to me—*here*!!" He struck his forehead sharply. "Listen," he hurried on, "I finished college—had a swell job all lined up in New York, commercial artist. They begged me to come back. One year, they said—put the place back on its feet. And I gave up my job." He suddenly screamed: "One year! Almighty God—I've been here six! Six years! I've given them six whole years!"

Dubé felt a grey misery mount up within him. Was this tragic dereliction to be his own fate? Had this been the fate of those others who had come up here to wrest a living from the earth?…But a curious change now swept over the younger man's face. He came close and clutched Dubé's arm convulsively, muttering brokenly.

"I must go! I've got to get away from here! I'm afraid…" He glanced behind him at the calf stretched in its pool of blood. A quick shudder went through him. "I—I'll go mad here if I stay much longer! It's getting me now. And I'm afraid, I tell you, afraid—*it might happen!*" He brought this out between clenched teeth, while he beat livid knuckles against his mouth, knuckles tightened over the half of the great knife. He looked at Dubé with a wild, indescribable expression.

Dubé stepped back, shook off the other's hand. His mind whirled in a chaos. He was hungry; an unutterable exhaustion made him want to fall where he stood, to sleep it didn't matter where. Even here horror was once more creeping upon him. Exerting himself to a great effort, he spoke: "What—what d'you mean?"

A voice from behind broke in. "Go in to dinner, you two," Scott said with his habitual good humor. "I'll finish up here. Be with you in a minute. Pop's makin' to sit down, and Annie's ready to serve."

Dubé found himself seated at a round, massive, old-fashioned table covered with a simple white cloth. A kerosene oil lamp with a frosted globe brought the table and the little group round it into pleasant relief. He sat next to old Nevin, who, with his back to the fire, fidgeted in childish excitement at the rare event of entertaining a guest.

"The bread, Annie," he called unnecessarily, for it was piled up behind the lamp. "And Scott, off with you and bring in the water pitcher...cut-glass," he confided to Dubé with pride as it was placed near him; "used only special, like. Annie, she don't let us folk use it. Last time it was nigh a year back, when...when...Dave, run in and bring the roast."

The savory odors that pervaded the room aroused in Dubé an almost painful expectancy. Dave, seated on his father's right, rose slowly, looked at Dubé for a flickering moment with an indefinable expression, shifting the glance to his father, then he moved away with sudden swiftness toward the kitchen. In the set of his mouth there seemed to lurk a curious exultation. Scott, busied at the table, looked up after him and called out, "Just a minute, Dave, it's not sliced yet."

Dubé saw him look significantly at Annie who nodded slightly and at once turned toward the kitchen. She had hardly taken a step when Dave stalked in abruptly, bearing a great platter on which reposed an immense round of meat, golden-brown and steaming. Intent, without a glance at anyone, he strode swiftly to the table and placed the dish before his father. A large fork and a glittering carving knife lay across one end of the platter. Annie stood quietly wringing her hands. Scott began a stumbling run round the table toward his father.

During several moments the old man stared, not at the platter, but only at the carving knife. His expression seemed to discredit what he saw. Then his face literally collapsed, working hideously with the dreadful mobility of the toothless. Scream upon scream, high split, was torn from his lips. "Take 't 'way—take 't 'way!" He pushed away from the table violently, shriveling back into his chair, putting up his arms as though to ward off a descending blow, and again beating them about violently. A convulsed black heap, he continued to scream and gabble until Scott picked him up like a child and carried him to the couch. There is lay trembling and moaning, feebly while Scott bent over him with reassuring words. In the meantime Annie hurriedly removed the great platter back to the kitchen.

Dubé, who had risen from his chair uncertain and perplexed, slowly sat down again. He was suddenly aware of Dave facing him across the table, a dark, sullen look of triumph upon his face.

"What—what's wrong?" Dubé asked him.

But Scott was beside his brother now, and for the second time that day his voice, though hushed, vibrated with fury. Yet there was in it a note of despairing appeal.

"Oh, you fool!...How could you do it—here, now?" But Dave seemed not to hear; he look steadily at Dubé with a frozen expression. Then all at once he stepped back, facing them all threateningly. Words began to pour from him in a torrent.

"I'm going to tell you something...And you lay off me with all that talk of yours, Scott. I've stood about enough of this nonsense...fed up to the teeth with this damned place anyhow! I'm through, see—*through!* And if you think—"

Annie interrupted as she came in placed a dish of the sliced meat on the table. "Never mind all that, Dave—tell it afterwards. Just sit down now, or all the supper'll be cold, and after all the fixin' I've been put to..." Her voice ran on gently, smoothly, with a kind of hidden force, holding easily to the gathered foreknowledge of a long lesson learned, like the slow, sure thrust of a river after a thousand miles of collected torture.

Scott pushed his brother toward a chair. "Sure, Annie, let's eat. We won't back down on you ! He looked over at his father. "How're you comin', Pop? Feel like a bite—heh?"

The old man mumbled, loosely sucking his lips back and forth.

Laboriously he scraped one leg after the other off the couch and pushed himself to a sitting position. All at once a wild, distraught look came into his face. He snatched off the black skull-cap, clutching his head with frantic hands.

"Annie...it's come, Annie!...The knockin'...the gallopin'...it's come!" Whimperings mixed with curious animal sounds bubbled from him as he rocked to and fro in an extremity of terror and misery. Scott quickly bore him from the room.

"Pop has these bad spells sometimes," he explained later. "He'll come through pretty soon. Too excited. Annie, pass the bread along."

Dave's eyes burned with fury. Bah! A pack of lies! But wait...wait...

Mechanically, without relish, Dubé ate what was placed before him. Not even the friendly efforts of Scott and Annie to banish the effects of the bizarre scene which had ushered in the meal could dispel the dark cloud that settled like doom upon his mind. David ate in silence, withdrawn and sullen, like a sinister presence that had forced an entrance to the company. He kept looking at Dubé covertly, as though a secret understanding lay bridged between them.

The desultory conversation shifted to Dubé and his immediate affairs. A tentative plan emerged. He was to use their team every morning to clear and plough his land until the arrival of his own from the old farm. The pruning must be done at once. Only a section of the large orchard was to be worked for the summer crop.

He agreed passively to the arrangement, without any gratitude. Somewhere far back he knew it was all a black deception. And quite suddenly he wanted to get out of this house, run away from these people who were trying to be so kind. Once more he felt the dear promises of human companionship dissolving. This house was just another lighted trap where men smeared the poisons hidden in their souls. Out in the darkness, surrounded by the illimitable night, he might stride, towering, free, as in the best days of the past, and shout to the friendly stars. Whatever happened he could always count on their being there... steadfast...eternal.

"Good-night"…"Good-night."

"Sure an' be around tomorrow…the team…luck."…

He moved up the drive without looking back and stepped out on the road. The confusion and darkness within him enveloped like a pall. He walked heavily, in a kind of trance, toward his own empty house. He was only dimly aware when footsteps came at him out of the night, running. As by some inner audition he was conscious of a voice, babbling, babbling, now rising savagely, now subsiding. In his mind a shutter suddenly fell and there was the dark, lupine face with eyes fixed, staring at him; the mouth worked silently, convulsively making words, words…Horrible!…But what was that?…He heard them now. The words rushed at him, leapt and beat about his throbbing head, suddenly resolved into frightful meaning and fastened upon his burning brain like a succubus.

Ah!… In a flash understanding came. So this was old Burt Nevin's secret?…When?…Nine years back?…With what?…A carving knife! No wonder the old man cannot stand…Oh! He saw it afterwards—the knife…But merciful heaven!—Why? …Ah…hunger! yes, trapped out there under the pines…three mounds…

But there was that dark face, silent now, leering, watching him. The face tilted back and a laugh, long, demoniac, broke out… Dubé, suddenly raging, lunged at it blindly…to smash it, blot it out….

Slowly he picked himself up where he had sprawled in the rough road. He was alone. He stood, unlistening, gazing into the blackness of the heavy timber on his right. When he stumbled forward again was it a spectral fancy that all the massed trees out there moved too? Moved like a tremendous rout of giants, lending the somber, comforting bulk of their presence, steadily, silently trudging the black distance into infinity…

Mechanically he turned into his own drive and entered the deeper gloom of the house; mechanically he lit the oil lamp and sank into a chair by the rickety table in the living room. Fumbling in his pockets, he drew out Bessie's letter by accident. Slowly he opened it and let his eyes wander along the lines idly, unseeingly. At the conclusion his eyes held on the name Bessie, under which were scrawled Virgie and Don. Aroused, he went back and read the letter. A tender emotion stirred briefly in him at the recital of familiar things. The children were eager to come. And Bessie spoke of "a new start". They would be with him in two weeks. What should he write back? How could he tell Bessie that... Oh God! Lies, lies!... He looked dully past the letter. Two weeks. Until then—work. Alone.

When he raised his eyes he caught his own reflection, together with the pale moon of the lamp, balanced there in the window; no, beyond the window. He gazed at himself as though in a dream, floating there detached, outside of time, deliciously suspended without feeling in another existence, purged of all weariness, all anxiety... The lamp guttered and flared, bringing him back with a shock.

In his utter exhaustion despair, like an iron hand, closed about his heart. Yet a deep uneasiness, quite alien to his despair, stirred with a muted vibration. It was the uneasiness of a mind in which some precise thought begins to take form in sensation: a kind of ganglionic telegraphy, a trembling of awareness dimly weaving along the nerves before erupting to its apotheosis of thought and deed.

Gradually the man slumped forward on the table, a grotesque and formless heap under the yellow light. The lamp burned on, and Jean Dubé slept.

Part III

A week went by—a cyclic trance of moments, moments divided between the cracking sinews of work, moments blind under the dreamless lapses of sleep. So long as Dubé kept his will stretched to the supreme violence of labor, he won a desperate courage from suspense.

Then—spring.

Spring came suddenly to the mountains. Like the instant relaxing of a grim face in the warmth of humor, it laid those indefinable touches that smooth away and round out, a preparation, when life wheels once more into the long friendly furrow.

Trills and flutings, doubled in echo, began to edge the sharp morning air. In the earth there began a stirring: blind tellurian impulses aching for the sun, reaching through grained tunnels for the ultimate benediction of heat.

Single-handed, Dubé flung himself at the earth in a mindless fury. With hunched shoulders, each hand a vice upon the plough handles, he stepped tirelessly, bathed in sweat, the great muscles of his back and thighs moving in faultless rhythm. The two horses glistened and steamed; straining, they whinnied and tossed their heads back as though uncertain as to what manner of creature held them to this frenzy of work. Their eyes started, their mouths were heavy and a-grin with the foam that flew, spotting their haunches in little white nodules. Yet, later, backing their stalls, they would feel reassured. The strong hands that groomed their dirt-stiffening coats held a thrilling knowledge of the sore muscles bunched with strain, smoothly kneading, loosening them for the next day's punishment.

Before the gleaming fang of the plough the earth boiled and gushed. And into that black loam Dubé poured his strength like a prayer, a prayer that must somehow rise again, sweep into a splendid antiphonal of fruitage.

Every day was a repetition of the last. The horses began to show signs of fatigue. And then one morning one of them threw a shoe. Dubé stood glumly wondering how soon it might be fixed. As he picked up the shoe a sound broke the stillness. At the end of the long row of peach trees that stretched toward the house a truck was suddenly framed. They had arrived.

Scrambling from the truck, the four children caught sight of him and ran up screaming, danced around him and pulled at his arms, laughed and chattered shrilly all together.

"Daddy!"…"Daddy!"…"How are you daddy?"…"Here we are!"… "O-o-o, such fun—nearly slipped over the edge, coming up." He smiled as they continued skipping about the shouting their delight. He lifted up the smallest one and went to meet Bessie. There she stood, waiting, wearing her old brown coat over a cheap print frock.

"Hello, Jean. Now stop it, you children. Virgie, take them off to play, will you?"

"Hello, Bess." He put down the child, leaned over and kissed her briefly. "Welcome home!" His arm moved in an extravagant gesture.

She glanced at the house, at the orchard, at the great piles of wilted brush and prunings heaped like pyres at the edge of the trees. Her eyes traveled up one long row that ended against a black wall of forest overshadowed by the rocky Bluffs. Like my life, she thought, and the bitterness of it was on her tongue. She looked steadily at the evidence of the gigantic labor he had performed. For me, she thought, for us. An overwhelming pity surged up in her for this man. With deep intuition she knew he would fail, that he had already failed, that his attempt to root his life with hers had been a terrible mistake. She saw all at once that he was a child of the wilderness, an intrinsic part of it, one with its slow stealth and its infinite reaches, a sharer in its wry secrets; that for this man to go against it was to lose the key to its wild codes, to betray himself. Oh Jean, Jean, a voice cried out inside her, you've tried…but this is the end. She lifted a hand and touched him, then brushed at the quick tears that sprang to her eyes.

"Why, Bess, don't—please don't." He put his arms about her and drew her close to him. "See now, the leaves will soon be out, then the buds, the flowers, and after that"—she felt his body tremble against her with a sudden urgency, and his voice went thick and husky—"after that the fruit. A paradise, Bess, a little—paradise."

She shrank away from his touch, and it was as though she had struck him. He stood there, separate, alone. His head suddenly ached; for a moment his skull became a steel cap, red-hot, that contracted on his brain. The pain of it stabbed and fell downward, lodged in his very bowels. At the same instant, with shocking irrelevance, a brilliant picture focused upon the screen of his mind. He saw three graves, the green lichen on their crosses, the dark shadowing pines. Rigid, with hands clenched, he stared at Bessie without seeing her. She must never know that…never. Dimly, his ears were only aware of the excited voices of the children exploring. The children—yes, there were the children. This was going to be a nice place for the children.

Terrified, Bessie watched the change pass over him. She forced a smile, a smile held by her mouth alone.

"You're tired, Jean. Looks like you've been working too hard. But it looks fine. Only let up and rest a bit."

He looked at her now. "Aye, Bess. The weeds were nearly as tall as the fruit trees." He laughed ruefully. "But we'll make a home out of this yet, eh, girl?"

She assented with relief. This was accustomed ground once more. Underneath she knew that he didn't believe it, that he was only arguing with himself.

They had known each other long enough to exchange lies safely. They pushed these at one another like debased coins, the innocuous small change of their daily existence. It had become a pattern of dull regularity: the set idiom for the emptiness and bitterness in their hearts. Like two beggars, squatting upon the common ground of habit, they cheated themselves and one another, bereft even of the sad criticism of ironic mirth. Their fundamental division lay between them like a disease, incurable, accepted.

Bessie went into the house, and Dubé moved off through the trees to return the team. He caught a glimpse of the children. Huddled together, they were silent, looking fearfully at the sagging old barn. A monstrous face, it seemed to give back their gaze, resentful, challenging. Dubé realized that he himself had avoided entering it.

He took the horses over and groomed them carefully. Dave, morose and brooding as ever, helped him to re-set the shoe with scarcely a word. Dubé admired without envy the fine orchard spreading around.

"You've got a fine ranch here," he said, just to break the silence between them.

"Yes, fine for them," Davie returned. "But I'm getting out of this God-damn place soon. They can run it without me."

Dubé looked at him inquiringly.

"Going up into Canada. Alberta."

Dubé's heart leapt suddenly. A great nostalgia swept over him; happy memories flooded through his mind. Freedom! If he could only catch back those great days, hunting and trapping across the boundless wilderness again. That was where he belonged.

"That was my country—once," he said.

The other looked at him sharply. "Was it?" he asked. "Maybe it can be yours again. By god!" he went on eagerly, "why not come with me? We'll go together. Here's your chance. Don't you have a right to start, to make another stake?"

"Yes, a chance," Dubé said evenly, a dull despair coming back,, "but not a right."

The finality in his voice made Dave turn on his heel with sharp vexation and stride away.

Old Nevin now appeared at the back door of the farmhouse and called to him. Bright and bird-like, the old man's eyes sought him out, seemed to pounce upon his visitor.

"Hey, hey, neighbor, there you are. Glad to see you. Folks come yet? Dubé nodded quietly. He liked the old man.

"Bring 'em over, neighbor. Let's see, today's Thursday. How 'bout Monday? Eh? Hey!, hey! Got to cel'brate the Spring! Bring 'em to dinner. Be looking for you. Sure! An' don't work too hard." He waved his stick, chuckling, his stubby beard wagging on his chest. Dubé smiled at him and strode up the drive to the road. Halfway home, he halted and sat down on the bank by the roadside. He sat there a long time, idly breaking twigs in his fingers and flicking them into the road. The pain came into his head again, crushing in upon his brain savagely.

A day slid by. Almost at once their life fell into the precise lines of routine; a routine that strengthened the illusion of safety and pushed back the tragic shadow of reality. There were moments, however, that began to recur with mounting frequency, when the bare truth of the situation was unmuzzled, thrusting itself forward through the wavering shroud of illusion like a naked snout. Among the hundreds of pictures that lay in Dubé's experience that of the three graves in the woods began to take precedence. His mind became a kind of palimpsest upon which the details of this picture flamed, burning out all others. He came to think of himself, curiously, as a man with a deck of cards: no matter where he cut the deck, the same card appeared. He said nothing about this or the pain in his head to Bessie. It was his secret. With a kind of exultation he became cunning, vaguely conscious of a duality that must be hidden within himself. He would be seized with guilt, which would then be replaced by a pleasurable sensation mixed with a touch of vanity.

The mornings were still given over to ploughing and dragging the soil in the orchard. Virgie at first followed the team, happily singing as she sank her bare feet in the damp, freshly turned earth. Then one morning she shouted excitedly, squirming with

"Daddy, Daddy—stop! Come see here! Look what I found!"

Dubé halted the team and obligingly came back. At her feet lay a huge white grub, wriggling and flexing its fat, crinkled body in an effort to burrow into the soil again. He regarded it steadily for several moments, then suddenly put his heel upon it.

"Bad for the trees," he said, as though speaking to himself, land stalked back to work. The little girl stood gazing down at that microscopic tragedy. It had really been such a funny, pretty little thing, twisting and flopping in the dirt. Why—? She looked after her father, a great puzzlement taking the place of the first shock. Still puzzled, and a little afraid, she left the orchard.

Thereafter Dubé worked alone. The four children either played near the house or trailed off into the woods across the road. They avoided going up to explore the precipitous Bluffs, contenting themselves with viewing the rocky eminence from a distance. Dubé was glad. His secret was safe.

Then, on the afternoon of a Monday they were to dine with the Nevinses, a strange thing happened. Dubé, having nothing to do at the moment, came idly round to the front of the house. As always, he moved silently. Virgie, on her knees, was busily scratching out a little bed with his jackknife, borrowed for the purpose. "We must have a garden, Daddy," she had said, shaking two packets of seeds. "Nasturtiums and daisies." He remained quietly looking down at her, amused at the fingers so nimbly plucking weeds. She worked quickly, oblivious of his presence. A minute went by. He stood motionless. At last he spoke, softly, dreamily.

"Are you making a garden?—poor little girl, poor little girl."

Startled, Virgie wheeled round, balanced squarely on hands and knees, staring up at him with wide eyes. She was like an animal, measuring an opponent, probing with its odd sense of delineation for the dangers latent. All at once she leapt to her feet, the knife flew clattering against the house-boards, and she fled screaming into the house.

Amazed, and puzzled in his turn, he hurried after her, to find the girl clinging to her mother and sobbing. To all their questions she only shook her head mutely, unable to give any explanation.

"You must have given her a fright, Jean," Bessie said. Slowly the sobs stopped.

Dubé wandered into the yard and began splitting wood, waiting for the family to get ready to go to dinner. At least Bessie called to him. He put down the axe.

"No, Bess. Headache. You go with the children."

She did not press him. "All right. You take a rest, Jean." She turned to the four children and inspected them critically once more. "No, Jeanette, you must leave Anna Belle. Daddy'll look after Anna Belle."

The little girl pouted and reluctantly put down the ugly, sawdust-filled doll, which was half her own size. Anna Belle, dirty, bedraggled and soggy, was her greatest treasure, guarded jealously, cared for with maternal solicitude.

After they had gone, Dubé picked up Anna Belle and dropped her on the rickety table in the living room where she lay in grotesque pantomime, one leg doubled under her formless body. He brought in the kerosene lamp and lighted it, carefully adjusting it against flaring.

For nearly an hour he sat quite still, his head resting in his hands. A spectator would have judged him asleep. Painfully he tried to resolve the confusion in his mind, to find a clear line along which to move. He fixed on the worst problem of all: food. For two days, now, every meal had consisted simply of rhubarb sauce and white bread. How long could this go on? The end was close, definitely in sight. Starvation. There was no one to whom he could go, and Bessie had no near relatives. The harvesting was still far off, and problematic. He had no truck, either to ship the crop to the depot thirty miles down the valley.

His mind circled these facts again and again, fumbling vainly for a solution, a way out. And then the pain stabbed through his head, a steel cap contracting, closing down upon his brain. He groaned and tore at his hair in an effort to relieve the agony; perspiration beaded out and ran down his face. Slowly the spasm abated, and he rose, moving about the room, looking out of the windows, touching objects without purpose. The hands of the cheap alarm clock that stood on a corner shelf crept towards nine. Still moving about the room, he caught a glint of light on the old text card hanging near, and for the first time halted and read it. His attention became instantly riveted, keenly alert. He took a deep breath and read again. His eyes followed the flourish of silver letters against the dark green, absorbing their full meaning.

> *They that be slain with the sword are better than they that*
> *Be slain with hunger: for these pine away, stricken through For*
> *want of the fruits of the field.*
>
>   *Lamentations 4:9*

Like a light in the distant window of a sanctuary, the idea shone clearly, beckoning to him. He moved forward thankfully as it rose up and invested his mind completely, familiarly, as though it had always been there. Of course; that was it. He had found his solution. It had been within reach all the time.

Dubé smiled and a cunning look came into his face. He glanced at the table, at the doll lying angular in the pool of light. Quickly he slipped into the kitchen.

The clock pointed to nine. Down the road Bessie and the children were returning home in high spirits. They had dined heartily. Soon they caught sight of the light in their window. Ben had a sudden thought.

"Sh-h!" he warned. "Let's sneak up and surprise Daddy." Like conspirators they tiptoes up the drive and crept to the side window. Bessie picked up Jeanette so that she, too, might enter into the fun. They peered into the room, bubbling with suppressed excitement. And suddenly their mirth was gone, their plan forgotten. Horrified, they stared into the lighted interior.

Dubé sat at the table, his face full in the light and profiled sharply against the further gloom. A great butcher knife flashed in his hand as he laid the edge on the shapeless neck of the doll stretched before him. With one swift stroke he swept the head from the trunk. The sawdust poured out upon the table. The mangled doll held the man's eyes as he instinctively wiped the blade on his sleeve.

The five watchers suddenly jumped and cowered down as the man inside started to his feet. The frail table rocked, nearly upsetting the lamp. He rushed across the room and tore the text from the wall.

"God!" he shouted, throwing his head back and lifting both arms in the air. "God! You, You have given me the sanction! Let it be on your own head now!" He broke into a peal of mocking laughter. "On your own head, God!" He flung the text derisively from him with all his force. Breathing heavily, he leaned against the wall, trembling, holding his head in his hands. Across the whirling chaos of his mind sped the blinding conviction of a brindled ferocity behind the order of things.

Outside, Jeanette began to whimper softly. Bessie moved swiftly now. In a moment she opened the front door, the three older children at her heels. She put Jeanette down.

"Virgie, take them up to bed at once. No, don't wait." As they groped their way in frightened haste to the single room upstairs, she turned to her husband. She was profoundly agitated, frightened, not knowing what to expect next. Without a word he went to the kitchen, drank greedily from the dipper, and lurched into the bedroom. When Bessie followed him later, she found him asleep on the bed, fully clothed. She remained awake, listening, thinking, wide-eyed in the darkness.

And she was still awake when the dream smote him. He twisted, moaned, making queer strangulated sounds in his throat. Then he lay quiet, muttering occasionally. She kept as still as death, shivers coursing through her body, wondering what was going on in the man's mind, what frightful shapes were given life in his sleep. One thing she knew, that she must be there ready to protect the little ones upstairs. For this she must steel herself for anything that might come. Somehow she must take them away from this terrible place that lay like a weight upon her day and night.

The man began to moan and thrash once more. Then, without warning, he bounded from the bed with a cry, and, awake now, rushed from the room to the kitchen. Terrified, she followed him at once. He bent over the rusty sink and poured water over his head. She felt that he grew calmer and a great relief flowed through when he spoke to her in a natural voice out of the darkness.

"Feel better now, Bessie. Just a nightmare."

"Come on, Jean." The steadiness of her own voice surprised her. "Let's get some sleep."

He fell asleep almost at once. Bessie listened to his quiet breathing for some time and at last drifted into broken slumber.

For several days after this Dubé moved about his tasks listlessly, as though preoccupied. Ten acres had been prepared for harvesting. Bessie watched him in all his comings and goings. She told Virgie to keep the other children near the house.

Jeanette refused to be consoled with the mended doll, and Anna Belle lay neglected in a corner. Once the child came into the kitchen when her father was there alone.

"I'm hungry, Daddy. Give me something."

He took out a loaf of bread and picked up the knife, When, a moment later, Virgie came in, she saw her father standing still and regarding the expectant child oddly, while his thumb gently tested the blade. She snatched the little one away in fear.

"If you want something to eat, you just come and ask me. Don't *ever* ask Daddy." She gave this warning after they had hurried out of earshot.

To Bessie the days wore the appearance of interludes in a melodrama. She dared not leave the place for a moment. They were effectually isolated here, living a life that narrowed down to the small stage of the house and its environs. Most of all she feared the nights, for she felt that danger approached close, stood in her room beside her, waiting for an unguarded hour.

And that hour came. It came with the recurrence of Dubé's terrible dream. He had not described this dream and she had not asked. But it returned, and once more the man moaned and tossed about while she lay tense, waiting. She felt her nerves would snap with the strain of this watching, and she made up her mind there in the darkness that, come what might, she and the children would leave the next day. She didn't care where they went so long as they were not encompassed by this accursed place. She would be quite content to sleep in the woods, or brush aside her pride and appeal to the Nevinses, humbly beg their help, their hospitality.

As before, Dubé at last vaulted from the bed with a shout, stumbled from the room through the kitchen, and literally collapsed on the kitchen steps. She came upon him there, rocking and holding his head with misery. A great pity for him almost pushed away her terror. He needed her help. She must do something for him, something…

"What is it, Jean?" she asked anxiously, her voice trembling. "Tell me. Tell your Bessie, please." She placed her hand gently on his head, sat down beside him and touched his forehead. Her hand came away wet.

He groaned and continued rocking himself. And all at once he was sobbing on her shoulder, words tumbling brokenly from his lips.

"The nightmare, Bess—the same—came back! It mustn't—I can't—stand it again. Keep it away, Bess… But you can't!" He suddenly cried out. "You can't. It's in here, see—in here." His hands went to his head; he put his face close to hers, speaking quickly. "I must tear it out, Bess, tear it out. It's the only thing." For a short while he fell silent, seeming to ponder this resolution. Then he went on.

"Listen, Bess, I'll tell you…the dream. There's a woman, see, a woman…up there on a ledge…head hanging over. And look…her throat…" He paused; then hurried on. "The blood is falling, falling. A great pool below…and people are coming, thousands of people… trying to reach it. But they can't…they can't. They struggle, fight, kill each other. Some scream…run away. A voice laughs…says to me, 'That's Life, Jean Dubé: Look at her. She pours herself out, but they don't know how to reach her gift. They will die hungry, the fools… always hungry!' And the voice laughs again." He gazed before him, trembling at the freshly evoked vision. "And it will come back, Bess, it will come back" Oh, God, I'm going mad, mad!"

Before the depth of his misery, Bessie felt powerless. There was nothing she could do. She thought of the children sleeping peacefully upstairs. A choking compassion for them filled her. My babies, she thought, poor little things.

When, some minutes later, she and Jean had returned to bed, Bessie felt drained of all strength, bodiless. Beside her the man breathed easily. Let him sleep…dreamlessly, was her only prayer. Tomorrow… tomorrow… Fold upon fold, sleep enveloped her exhausted mind and body. Outside, rain began to fall, sibilant, lulling.

Bessie wakened with every sense alert. Scarcely breathing, she waited, listened. Fear clamped upon her mind. She knew with acute certainty that she was alone in the room. Rain. A thin spicule of sound came for an instant. She knew that sound: one of the kitchen drawers. The knife, she thought, he is taking the knife. She felt she couldn't move. An eternity passed before she heard a stair board creak. Ah, he was going to do it! But there was still time. No, she must not scream. Quiet, and courage, only courage. Her body became galvanized. Suddenly she was strong again…

Upstairs, that thin spicule of sound had caught Virgie's ear. She lay stiff on the straw pallet, listening. She rose and stepped to the window, looked out for a moment at the dim rain, turned back to the room listening to the measured breathing of the three others. She flattened herself on the floor and stared down the dark well of the staircase. Fright held her in a trance, and she began to cry silently.

Then he reached the stair. One…two… The third stair creaked and the man paused. She wanted to shriek, to gather the children and fly, but she could not. They were all trapped. She heard another sound, and knew her mother was coming.

"Is that you, Jean? Where are you going? Let the children sleep. Come down now; bring me a drink. There's no water in the kitchen." Her voice sounded strong, persuasive.

Dubé turned uncertainly on the stairs, looking down at the dim figure of his wife.

"I must, Bess. It is the only way. God Himself has willed it. They will starve. We cannot see them starve, Bess…Oh my God! My God!"

Virgie listened. Behind her the children began to str. They must never know this…never! Quietly she moved from one to the other, soothing them with soft sounds. Her mother's voice came again, pleading, arguing, demanding. The girl knew that her mother was fighting a battle for their lives in that lonely house. She hardly recognized her father's voice as it came up now.

"Though I lose my soul I will save them from starvation. Poor little babies…my poor children. Little Virgie, she will never know… Starvation and death here alone. The butcher knife is sharp and there is no bread to cut…. My poor little babies!... Someone will find us all and bury us in the orchard. Oh my God! My God!"

"No, Jean. God has not forsaken us. Tomorrow Scott is coming with money. Come, lie down awhile and I'll get you a drink of water."

She talked on, still pleading, arguing. Presently Virgie heard the padding of bare feet moving away. The voices receded to vague whispers. The room once more became a field of night. A door closed downstairs, and her mother came hurrying up.

"Your father," she said, "he's gone." She lay down beside Virgie till a sickly grey light widened in the room.

An hour later she and the children had reached the Nevins' farmhouse. With Scott she turned back in search of her husband. The rain had ceased, and heavy mist funneled up the valley, pouring over the mountains, swirling thickly about the searchers. Before long it began to thin, and they found themselves near the iron-bound ridge of White Horse Bluffs.

In the white welter of scudding clouds the dark spine of the Bluffs heaved, alternately loomed and vanished like some fabulous monster flanged and hooded with steel, driving into vast continents of spume, plunging tremendously through the silver drift of seas.

They found him at last, sprawled across the three graves under the pines, his throat cut. All about them, the trees stood silent, remote, darkly aloof from the spectacle of human grief.

The Forest Pool

A Parody of Love

It chanced that two men once met in a forest, and both agreed to take the same path together until such time as their journeying should part them asunder.

The tongue of one had many forkings, but that of the other was quiet, and his soul ran swift and straight. The laughter of one called fright and amazement into the soft eyes of the beautiful forest creatures; but upon the lips of the other speech became a fine music, and in his soul wisdom dwelt in the true laughter of silence. Thus each in his separate wise beguiled the way with strident mirth, with sprightly tale, and with thoughtful word.

By and by they stepped aside to find a resting place and to partake of food, for the shadows had stretched and the travelers were hungry. Moving through a cool glade with branches arching far overhead, of a sudden they came upon a pool whose calm waters slept in a breathless trance of shadow and sunlight. Both men stood rapt in the stillness of wonder, struck by the surpassing beauty of the pool. And looking upon its beauty, each in his way saw it to be infinitely desirable.

"True desire," said the wise one, "is to touch life with the magnificence of love, and then to pass on into mystery."

But the tinkler of words understood him not.

"Ah," said the latter, "I must leave a token of myself here ere we move on." And thrusting a rude hand into his pocket he scattered a handful of chaff upon the smooth surface, making ugly the lovely face of the water. But a light wind danced through the glade and blew the chaff to the edge. Again, and yet again, did he fling careless chaff upon the water. But always the wind blew it away, leaving the pool to shine like a dark, polished jewel.

And the wise one, watching, said never a word. Slowly he sank upon the earth and gazed long at the beauty above and caught for a moment the flash of a foundered beauty held in the inscrutable heart of the pool. And he thought: "Here indeed will I leave an exquisite memory held forever in radiance and grace."

Now, working swiftly, upon the loom of imagination he spun the rare fabric of a great thought; into the thought he wove the magic of a marvelous design, strange with the twin threads of Love and Sorrow. And when he had finished he called it his Dream; and taking it, he weighted it with a bit of Wisdom, and watched as it sped like a fairy meteor through the unspeaking depths. There it lay at last, far below, glowing softly in a transcendent loveliness.

And forever after travelers would pause here to rest and look upon the growing beauty of the pool. Sitting as though in a trance, they would gaze at the wondrous glow far beneath, wherein seemed to gather all the shining dreams of their troubled and weary lives. Then, touching their lips to the cool water, they would pass on their way, each to his long accounting.

Poems

Sonnet

(Evening Fantasy)

When Night, the nurse, lulls Day's fair child to sleep,

And night-winds breathe a voiceless lullaby,

Long shadows, like a secret maiden shy,

Unlace soft glories that, unbidden, peep

From mist-veiled valley and from rock-girt steep.

And as the huddled forms of night draw nigh,

Dark Cybele, tumultuous once with sign,

Runs strepitant, high revelry, to keep.

Darkness!—and faintest flash of fairy wings—

The sunset dreams of mortals swift in quest

Of dewy meed to still sad questionings

That brim to quiv'ring lips and bring no rest.

Ah, love! Thus do our dreams new pleasures drink

From Hope's deep goblet, nevermore to sink!

(Colgate University, November 26, 1923)

Sonnet

(Man and Life)

What towering mountain-barrier yet has stayed

The golden eagle's heaven-assailing flight?

Yet, God! What a gulf is every starry height

To Man's imperial mind, immortal made!

What bounded void of Earth has yet displayed

Such boundless wastes of soul? Caves of the night!

Gorged hells of sophistry!—Yet, with the light,

What rush of giant wings up Heaven's stern grade!

Life's sea hath shores that no horizon fleck,

And we put out serene, a-thrill to song.

Going we know not whither; only we hear

The siren-call of unseen glory. Wreck!

And after the night of storm a kneeling throng

In prayer: cold lips, hushed voices, and—a tear.

(Syracuse University, March 1924)

Sonnet

(Peace is Best)

Serene I look into your eyes, and calm,

Glad that the blood frees no delirious rain

Along the flaming highways of the brain.

Where passion brims the cup with bitter balm,

And reason drains the hemlock to the lees.

I am content that I your hand may hold

Sit with you here, and watch the subtle fold

That flows in silken ripples to your knees.

I know that peace is best—but when night's spell

Has woven magic veils, old memory

Calls like the long roar of the fluted shell:

I feel again your touch, your face I see

I breathe the necromancy of your name,

Find your identity in flower and flame!

(Redlands, CA)

Sonnet
(To Psyche–Absent)

My dearest, now that we are far apart

Through jealous hatred and the poisoned wiles

Of men, I fear my words—though from my heart

Of hearts—will only move vague memoried smiles.

For how can my most cunning script replace

The timeless measure of one folded kiss?

How may my thoughts, with finest fretted grace,

Catch my soul's vibrance voiced in passionate bliss?

Can all the march of words across my page

Call back that night of singing pulse, of lips

That found millenniums but a moment's age,

Of love's dear rites and deep companionships?

All fear were empty, did I know you true;

Yet trust must be my text—since I LOVE YOU.

(March 18, 1931)

Sonnet
(To Psyche)

Once I remember how you came, all shy,
Stood slim before me with your eager glance,
Sheer in your Parian whiteness, in a trance
Of dear delight and glad expectancy.
And for a space of secret, radiant talk,
We laughed, and told the endless beads on Love's
Enchanted rosary, swore we would walk
Like ancient mystery in Attic groves.

At last, with swelling hearts, hand tight in hand,
You pledged sweet promise--yet sharpest fear, like nettles,
Stabbed sudden pain: you plucked a rose, near-blown,
Loosed, in a cloud, a moment's storm of petals!
May you not loose that Judas-blade, that word
"Farewell"—Love's lean, Love's dread misericord!

Sonnet

(Futility)

A cigarette burns slowly to grey ash,

The white smoke curling ceiling-ward as do

The hopes of honest men. Ah, if they knew

How truly hope must lead to pain; but rash

Fools ever hope; the wise are they that dash

Each human spark while yet the flame is blue

And hot, as when the thought was born. Subdue

Ambition! Do not build, for buildings crash!

One hour ago this cigarette lay white

And slender—beautiful! But when it sought

The flame which gave it life, drank eagerly

And deep of hopeful fire, to catch its light

Grey ash is witness to Futility!

(November 19, 1931)

Sonnet
(En Passant)

My dear, there are no better words that I

May find can clearer tell my love holds true

Then all those scented rhymes I've writ to you

To lock within your heart's strong treasury.

All thoughts of you burn like rare gems that frame

Deep in their gleaming worlds your memoried face;

Nor time, nor change, nor yet the bitter grace

Of sorrow can erase your graven name.

Into the mists of Silence you have drawn,

Yet ere yon white oblivion steal with soft

And cunning hand to veil love from your eyes.

Remember still a little while there's one

Who pledged his heart in many a line and oft

To dare new worlds with you in Love's emprise!

(Seattle, April 17, 1931)

THE UNREDEEMED

You are the soldiers;

We, you say, the sleeping dead

Lulled in the mounded peace of earth,

All accounts quite squared, balanced

Cancelled from the books of life,

Debt and debtor one.

We girded for bright accolades of fame

And won a grim gratuity of teeming crosses,

Soaring monuments in city squares.

And now we sleep, you say, in peace

Deep in our sharded cenotaph of mold,--

Aye! Clipt fast, trenched, ribbed, sealed,

Flinted down, bastioned by the reeling centuries!

The dead know well

How lips and love and lust

Are regimented with the dust.

We have forgotten, we have quite forgotten

The wandering touch of wind upon our cheeks;

The surge of color down old summer glades;

Red sunsets scumbled on the palette of the night;

Light-shaken waters flooding to the sun

And Amphitrite cruising in her silver shell.

Forgotten the bite of frost; the storied blaze

Of winter fires; the long sea-searching of the tides

For truth, the master-pearl, ledged beneath

The deep abysm of things.

And love—

Poor love!—

Shriven with the brimming chrism of sorrow.

All these we had, all these are gone,

Gone like sun-motes with the nascent dark,

Gone like phantom sigils on the broken

Urns of song. Do we lie here forgotten,

Listening to the cool and healing rain

Pour for millenniums?

O Unknown Soldier—enough! Come down!

Though you may sentinel a thousand years

Gray with the dust of heedless passing feet,

Blind to the sun, with eyelids ridged

Against the rain—

Your witness is in vain.

Again the armored legions roll, the guns awake,

Men stare along the steel to death

And iron heels drum on our fallen mouths.

Thermopylae! ... Austerlitz! ... Mons!...

And myriad other sounding names through whose

Enormous pulse runs swiftly the underdrum

Of blood and violence…

Bitter the shame, and bitter the fee! O Christ,

You who tune the golden wires of song

In churches shrill with the scrannel voice of creed,

Is this the peace that passeth knowledge,

To kiss again the cruel rood, play out again

Our blood-diced lottery with Death

Against some quickening dunelight in the soul?

O living comrades marching in the sun,

You are the soldiers,

Are we but the sleeping dead,

Lost pilgrims on the unreturning way?

For us it matters not,

Wind fast the shroud, seal fast the troubled lips.

Let lob-worms feast and tunnel in the clay.

Hope, like a star-shell, roams the night

And sinks back toward the dark.

Yet see! Bethesda lies in trance.

Strange wings are passing over!

(First published in *Interim,* a literary quarterly, 1945)

(Untitled)

1

When in your eyes, I glimpse the light

That burned in other days,

I know you long for yet another sight

Of faces that have gone their various ways--

Scattered like leaves upon the winds of Time;

While you alone, alone must climb!

O do not weep! The ghosts

Of other days have tears enough

To drown their eyes in dread, unlidded sleep!

I know I set more store by you

Than in the casual friend I meet

Upon the dusty street.

2

When you have gone away, I find

The best of me has gone with you.

The rest of me that stays behind

Does all the things I have to do:

Says all the words, smiles and laughs,

Ears and sleeps, and even writes

A score of jolly paragraphs

That never mention lonely night.

3

The Pigmy and the Giant ran

A startling marathon,

The course was set and soon they met

The avenue upon.

What though the traffic barred their way,

What though the Cops did frown,

Nor Medes nor Persians would have stayed

The laws from lost renown.

4

Betide nor where the white winds of our lives

May scatter us. Come, stand breast to breast,

And from our joining lips let fall one gem,

One little kiss, one tiny charity

For love's dear sake, to keep forever is

The treasur'd urn of sweetest memory.

If you but grant this humble boon I ask

Then would I take your quiet hands in mine.

Yea! Kneel before your radiant comeliness,

You, whom my passionate, insurgent heart

Has sought unceasing through these brightening days…

But should it not befall, remember this:

We will not wound each other

With careless word or name:

To you it was but 'friendship,'

To me it was—a flame!

(Seattle, WA, May 27, 1931)

5

I met you first within the whirling dance,

A thing of eager-clinging scarlet silk;

With knee to knee and vibrant breast to breast—

Flame-sped against the purple of the night,

One in the shimmering grace of movement bound to music.

6

They say a good time's comin'

But it seems damned far away

With its borders hung in purple mist,

Its lake in silver spray.

When the statue we call Liberty

Is a crumblin' heap o' bricks,

And the stooges—now our leaders—

Are deader then their tricks,

Why, <u>sure</u> a good time's comin'

It's a-lollopin' this way;

But the thunder of his golden hoofs

Is a million moons away:

That time is comin' sure as hell,

But savvy this, my boys:

You're getting' off your hunkers <u>now</u>

An' puttin' up your toys,

You're strappin' on your thinkin' box

Yeah, noodles filled with chow;

You're kickin' in the teeth of all

Who'd try to stop you now.

But what're you doin' for the Ship o' State

With her riggin' cut to hell?

She's takin' it green o'er the starboard bow,

She's takin' it green in the swell:

Is it "Hard a-port!" with the Leftists

With Stalin a-grin at the wheel?

With Marx a-flippin' the pancakes

And red syrup at every meal?

7

Life holds no glory now for me;

It is but ashes…dust…a lonely sea

Of bitter tears that, sullen, break

Upon the moving sands of desolate shores.

8

Now you are seventy-three

And I am that—plus seven!

Yet we are still together, Love,

Still in our own dear heaven.

The years have come and gone

The days like chaff are driven

But we have braved all weather, Love,

To rim with gold our heaven!

9

How curious that the crusty crane

Honks moonlight down the wintry skies,

With zodiac stare in cosmic train,

Above the whistling golden eyes.

Great tireless wings that cleave the night

White-pronged above the moonlit plain,

Bound for far lacrustine rite,

Deep-seeded dream within the brain.

Slow Stain

A sin, you say?--At sixteen?

Why, had you but seen--Well, she stood there

White and shining; tossed the word, careless;

Laughed "Of course!"—sudden—like that:

And smiles had danced enticements on her lips

(You should have seen her, sir!)

As she went flashing on her airy way.

Ah, yes, a jest. But time...the years...

You see, the word had fallen

In that silent circle--surely caught!--

And glances leapt in the green flash

Of guarded hate.

What further? Well, she went--

You remember Grindel's Poole?...And see,

There leans her stone, that moss-grown one;

Her crimson lips have drunk their dark eternity!

Subliminal

I am your latest dream

All gold and amber-bright,

A shining cloak of truth

To gird your sleep with light.

You bade me come. I came--

Slowly, groping, blind,

Reeling across the ledges

Of your tunneled mind.

But see, my dear, these wounds...

Here...and here...and here:

The knives of Memory

The gleaming spikes of Fear!

In me you forged a courage

Wry with honesty;

In me your lifted banner

Dared infinity!

(November, 1937)

Waterfront

Night

The city sleeps. Somewhere moves

The soaring amplitude of song

While night-trucks thunder down the waterfront.

Below the dock the drift sucks in and out--

The wash and crool of worn and sodden punk.

A cat creeps out to sniff a stranded fish head,

Crouches, frozen eye to eye at that sightless

Challenge of the deep.

Morning

Gulls, flaked upon the steel black sea,

Float, then dark with dream-swift wings

Conquering forever the unconquerable tides.

O Sea, your streaming flags hold no appointed truce

Though all your risen armies fly them

White against the main.

To A Pretty Waitress

Just one word as I go my casual way
And you go yours:
That somehow in your world of strident noise,
Coarse jests, and aching feet, you often pray
With a sense of deepest yearning for the joys
Of love and laughter flung on morning skies.

It may be that beneath your smiling eyes
Lurk tears and pain;
And all these fools who eat and drink and leer
Are nails sunk deep into your daily cross
To crucify your love of all things dear.

And so perhaps I shall come back again
Some other day
To find your tears too bitter even for weeping,
Your smiling glory drowned in pain,
Your treasured dream of love too bruised for keeping.

To A Good Neighbor
(Mr. Moore at 93)

Birthdays have a happy way

Of giving us the chance to say

Things that we might hesitate

To say on any other date.

It's nice to call you neighbor,

To pause from bended labor,

And quite a valued privilege

To chat awhile across the hedge.

(1969)

To Roslyn and Glen Jr. at 50

Lines

Now that you are fifty

And youth wears other face,

Let mill-race Time flow gently

Through fields of golden grace.

(October 2, 1979, May 6, 1984)

Beholden

I know you think me silly—

You hate my fuckin' neck—

But what does all that matter

Since you took my fuckin' check?

For money talks a lingo

The goddam world knows well,

A baleful Esperanto

That's known from heaven to hell.

Forbearance

I saw a hungry bird swoop down

To raid my garden bed;

He stretched a worm; I stretched a point,

And let him stay instead.

A Christmas Prayer

To those who yearn a Higher Life

To abdicate all sin, all strife,

Who groom their virtues with the balm

Of Holy Writ and lisping psalm,

And preen with sly and secret boast

At elevation of the Most!

That now their hearts, so clean, so free,

May close all deals (at higher fee)

To them, dear Lord, dispense thy favor,

As, kneeling, they salvation savor

Before thy Presence, Paraclete,

With honeyed prayers and piteous bleat,

Then smugly rise to shuffle out—

Come, flay their backs with whip and knout!

A Commission

You who have known the ache of grief,

That bitter minting of dear honesty

Coined from the blanch'd alchemy of tears,

    I charge you straight:

See that no traitor of betrayal lurks

In your dark garden of Gethsemane!

After soft names, no strident words unkind;

After white fingers, no stained hands uncouth;

After dear pledges, no Shylock-barter of the mind;

After joined lips, no ravished fans of Truth!

A Golden Parting

When darkness falls upon the tryst of life

    Then you and I

We take our different ways,

Rich with the glow of deep-companion'd days;

And parting, mark, with kindling eye

    And quiet clasp of hand,

How sudden from behind some western cloud

    The sun bursts out

To shower soft gold about our feet:

    For one wing'd moment

    Fields are ancient fire!

    Every hill a golden palace,

    Every tree a spire!

Old friend, goodbye! How high the trumpets call

To break our ranks within the courts of pain!

Who know but in some rare New Day,

Shrill golden trumps will close our ranks again!

A Petition

Oh, should you have some healing balm to pour

Upon my soul to give it wings to soar,

In eagle-flight we'd climb

to love's chartless sublime!

(Then fold me to your quiet breast

Like a homing bird that's found its nest,

Where I may sleep, where I may sleep!)

Should you reveal one word that will endure

The strength of living days—O come! Be sure

And whisper soft for me

Love's necromantic fee!

(Then loose! Untwine! Unbind, unbind!

And cover me till I am blind

Beneath your hair, beneath your hair!)

(June 10, 1931)

A Thought For......

Should this day, with its gold, be lost to me

I only hope that somewhere, o'er the hills,

You may have garnered something of its wealth

All yellow-sheav'd and hoarded for the deep

And shining hour when you and I again will meet.

An Impression

I'll not forget the night you stood

Scarce keeping back your tears—

Your glance fell to your reaching hand,

You whispered "Just six years!"

Pain has its monumental hour,

Its lone Gethsemane;

I learned it from your lightest word,

I caught it in your eye.

I know that in your laughter

Life cuts this epitaph:

"Love was her crucifixion—

A broken cross her staff."

(March 3, 1931)

Argument

1

You say that we must part,

Yet in the touch of flying fingers

You have spoken all your heart.

Your lips, you say, are sealed—

But eyes, dear love, flash star-lit trails

No sweet deception ere concealed.

You say you can't be mine—

But lips are rosaries of richest lies,

And kisses, love, their richest wine!

2

We nearly parted, love

That year, long gone;

For each to each we brought

Unmarrowed bone.

Yet had you left me, Love,

I would have followed;

I could not bear to live

With heart so hollowed.

But with forgiveness, Love,

We found each other;

And wisdom taught us, Love,

To work together.

A Wish

If I could be a cumbly-boo,

(But <u>not</u> a surly snarly-yow!)

I'd climb your gate, be nearer you,

Defeat the medics with a <u>pow</u>!—

Make even God eat crow!

For with my secret magic touch

I'd change the sorry frame of things

And metamorphose (in the clutch!)

A miracle of radiant wings—

A lord of air and space.

Then, Merlin-wise, we'd soar away

From smog and dust and killing heat

To nectar cups that brim all day

Where every breath's a heavenly treat

In gold fields of ecstasy!

(January 24, 1982)

At The Ritz

They come—a drift of color and a waft of scent,

Her husband—sleek, bloated architect of sin—Pompous, hat in hand,

With dislocated tie and grim with pique.

(How I hate men with pumps that squeak!)

He leans and breaks a flower for her;

Unlicensed fool! Of course he'd pin it to her breast

And fumble, with pretense, its soft allure and subtle rondure.

His fork is vagrant as his eye

Which now is swimming in champagne—

And see, it's on her throat again!

Birthday Thoughts

It has been said of married bliss

That love expires from kiss to kiss.

Can this be true

Of me and you?

For forty years your lips divine

Have kept distilling heady wine

For which I've found no anodyne!

How different the argument

If Fate had been on mischief bent.

But when you came

Without a name

And yelled to drown the doctor's ploy:

"It is a girl!" (O heavenly joy!)

<u>But what if you had been a BOY!</u>

(March 18, 1975)

Broken Dream

I've waited, parched with thirst for ecstasy

O lover-girl

These many days:

And made of Time a white expectancy

Against that meeting-hour of grace

When I should kiss your upturned face

In love's amaze.

Your silence turns our pledge to aching jest

And bitter rue!

My secret Scheme

To find love's sacrament, love's kingly best,

Is shattered like a lovely rose

That falls, in perfumed death, to close

Its broken dream!

(Sent to Glen, Jr. at Yale, 1954)

Christmas Cheer

I cannot wish you Happiness

(A niggling dame, I hear),

Not yet invoke a Merry face

When Harvard is so near.

When all along with Eli Yale

You tread the campus drear

With beetles, bugs, and driving hail

To bite and lash your rear—

Oh then, my boy, you'll hear the wheels,

Those dismal discs of Woe,

For Christmas, like a great black HEARSE

Comes grinding gaunt and slow.

Perched high upon the dicky sits

The liveried coachman, Fear,

And in his hand a bull-whip cracks—

Its name is Greed, my dear.

The straining mokes, two, have a name,

Their monikers you've met:

For one is Peace, the other Joy,

Twin steeds that share one sweat.

By now you'll think your only friend

Lives in your own brown attic:

He smiles at X and laughs with Y—

Unfailing Mathematic!

But Fear and Greed and Peace and Joy

Are names of Paradox—

With two of these we add your love

To goodies in this box!

(Sent to Glen Jr. at Yale for Christmas, 1954)

Could I But Know

Could I but know

The swift, victorious thought

That moves, proud rank on rank, uncaught,

Behind the mystery of your white

Marmoreal brow,

Then might I find, ere Death's dart sings,

The shining wonder of humility;

And honesty, unfettered with disguise;

Love, too, unglozed with silly tricks of pride;

And old Earth-wisdom, whose first truth's in being unwise;

And how frail Beauty, wrought into all lovely things,

Endures beyond Time's ruthless fee,

Returning—immortality!

Culture–Modern Style

Lymphatic is the freshman mind

When it begins the college grind.

Its culture is that Lydian thing

(Hark! I hear old Milton sing!)

A college yell—or else a ring

(Yes, Bell system—maybe Mr. King!)

The Soph—my word!—is such a spark,

Not <u>up with</u>—just <u>out for</u> a lark!

He plays the hard, expensive game

Of making for himself a name;

We strive to find the hidden grace,

But all we see is—just a face!

The Junior, with his two year's lore,

Oft finds that even thought will soar;

And dreams (as bowed with looks profound

He goes his quaint amoeba-round)

Of brushing up his mathematics

At the Triangle—with dramatics!

Dinner a la Tacoma

1

I edge into a booth to dine

While plates come wheeling into line;

With gastronomic airs divine

Come chickens, steaks, and gobs of swine—

(Oh, pardon!—'pork' is what I meant:

Stop—can't you tell it by the scent?)

2

Now comes a portly mutton chop

With succulence the breath to stop,

To sit in massive pride and drop

A curtsey—throw a carnal sop.

(Come pour the catsup's flaming tide,

The gates of appetite fling wide!)

For Flossie

O beautiful Dear,

Were you but here

The moment would be perfect to commune!

We'd turn sly time into a laughing-stock;

And sitting here at ease with you

We'd talk and laugh the night-long through—

As once we did, till morning dew!

And know there's nothing that we may not

Talk about

That finds not all the wisdom of the earth

Because you comprehend.

O beautiful Friend!

En Passant
(To Flossie)

As petals fall like clouds of perfumed tears,
So parting words drift down upon our heart;
Deep thoughts lie hidden from the curious gaze
Where pick nor mattock may the sense amaze.
Dreams sweet today turn bitter on the morrow—
Bitter as the ancient wells of Marah!
So ever is love's close, love's sad decline.

Now you have passed, it may not be the same
Again…and yet…but who knows the account
When swift the flick'ring sword of attitude
Has cut the lightning-threads of love that leap
From central gulfs of Being?
Yet if you will,
Come once again and take my hands, and leave
One kiss to call our own, no matter what.

In Aureum Memoriam
(To Flossie)

Thanks for the fifty golden years

We've bowled along together,

Through laughter, grief and faceless fears,

Through storm and golden weather.

We never had the Golden Touch

Poor Midas claimed of old,

A fool who asked a 'touch' too much:

Love seldom beds with gold.

Through golden rain and golden days

Our Wisdom Tree has spread

To bear the golden fruit of love

And bless your golden head.

Down golden road and shining plain,

Through thunder and through dust,

We'll climb through sunshine and through rain

Up where the gold stars thrust!

Ghosts

Though you are far away tonight, reach out
A gentle hand. I need your strength to keep
The peace you gave me, help me put to rout
Dim ghosts that walk and will not let me sleep.
Old wraiths of half-forgotten loneliness
That I had thought to bury when you came
Are haunting me till I must needs confess
I knew them once, and they are still the same
Who tortured me so long…. O agony
Of love remembered that can come no more!
O pain that follows after ecstasy
When time has set her lock upon the door!

My dear, my dear, reach out to me I pray
And let your love turn all the ghosts away.

Inheritance

I am afraid, who fall unseeking heir
To fettered tenure of an old estate,
Gray heritage of lowly as of great
Ruined by some, by others made most fair.
Within vague borders lie dense woods, and bare
Spine-barriered desert; rivulets their freight
Of reedy coolness bring, and dark stagnate
Green pools unfathomed 'neath a poisoned air.

Sometimes by day, but oftener seen by night,
There stir vast scaly Longings, dragon-eyed;
Pale Aspirations climb their starless height;
Gorged Satisfactions wallow in their mire.
I am afraid, whose greenest coverts hide
Their tawny Namelessness, with eyes of fire.

Last Words

When I gone,

think not of me as dead;

Only remember

Brave words proudly said.

Turn grief into

The ringing coin of joy

That neither moth nor rust

Can e'er destroy.

Embrace, dead love,

The warm spindrift of laughter;

Close fast the door

On dark days following after,

Our pledge of love

Was forged in linkless chain,

A golden gossamer that's held

Through loss and pain.

And now, beyond the flow

Of tide and time,

Our love, a matchless amaranth,

Lives on, sublime!

Lesson

O rose, sweet rose,

You float your scent upon the wind

Distilling comfort into aching hearts.

You breathe no pain,

You give no hint

When even with canker at your core

You lavish sweetness without stint

To teach the lesson of the Spartan lad again.

Lines for ---

Between the darkness and the light

Our words have been but few,

Yet rich the crystal cup of hours

I brim with thoughts of you.

Swift silence gilds with eloquence

Your lovely looks in bliss

That lips the milk of memory;--

May love peak more than this?

The dearest worth that in you stirs

Craves neither alms, nor word,

For rising words like bubbles burst,

The deeps lie pent, unheard.

No curious sword of insight probes

The mystery veiled in You;

No day can die quite songless now

That I have found you true!

A flake of moonlight, once you lay,

All silver dashed with jet,

And a secret, dear, your eyes unmasked—

But I forget…forget?

(February 19, 1931)

Lines To A Stye

Much has been sung of marble brows
And much of radiant eyes,
But never a word and never a line
In praise of radiant styes.

O mystic hump that blears the eye
And screens the edge of sight,
Protruding with unhallowed glow—
Tumescent anchorite!

Aloft you raise your painful peak
To make the proud world dim;
To subtlest glance of love's absurd
Across your flaming rim.

You rise in high and rufous glee
To play your dubious role,
Rubescent in your churlish pride—
Half-brother to the mole.

Upreared in blood-plumed majesty

Come, pay your final toll,

Ripe for the caustic price of Fate,

Grim Paracutin of the soul!

December, 1951

Lines to Marion

Birthdays have a happy way

Of giving us a chance to say

Things that we might hesitate

To say on any other date.

I met you on the passing wings of chance

(A daughter of the land of dike and fen),

A radiance on the summer air,

A shining globe of thistle-down

Seeded with laughter, joy and love.

You have edged the grayness of my days with light;

I quicken at your step, your knock; am happy just

To see your face, your smile, your steady eye.

And in the closing tumult of my after years,

I take your hand, embrace you, call you friend,

And give you what I have of love once more.

Love

This is the Gate—the Palace Gate,

    With Seal upon the Latch;

O Rider from the world of men

    Wherefore such swift dispatch?

Save with the Password's cryptic lore

    No entry gain you here,

Though you be faint with thirst, and sore

    With riding fast and far.

Now yield me but the Magic Word

    Then may you break the Seal;

And know, yet ere your lance be couched,

    You bring both Pain and Weal…

In richest Chamber of the Court

    The Banquet now is spread;--

Yet look you, Knight, remember straight;

    Let Heart keep faith with Head!

(Seattle, July 26, 1931)

My 'Friendly' Neighbor

My neighbor is a thundering bore,

And when he cocks his head and leers

I <u>know</u> what he will say <u>before</u>

He says it. Enough! I'm bored to death:

    What chance for friendly basis

    With a mind in frozen stasis?

What dribbles from his mind as wit—

(Forgive my bitterness, O Lord!)—

Is unadulterated s—t

To skid him to his last reward:

    A sad anthology

    Of rank scatology.

Yet once this quondam paladin

Climbed poles, strung wires without a hitch,

Ate food, drank Scotch, caught terrapin

And sired two furies on a bitch,

    Two Erinyes in loveless beds,

    Unblemished virgin maidenheads.

This Solon of the rheumy eye,

There's nothing that he doesn't know;

The lexicon of knowledge..why!

That's kindergarten stuff, below

    This <u>a priori</u> mind

        Lodged in his lean behind.

"Live and let live" the virtuous chelp;

But all such cant just leaves me cold.

Let Satan cheer, St. Peter yelp,

I must be firm, I must be bold—

I'll just load up my trusty gat,

Write 'Finis" on this odious rat!

Nocturne

I love this silent-flowing tide of dusk,

This flood of dark swept to the heart of Night!

And look! The moon juts like a silver tusk

Behind the many-shoulder'd mountain height.

Here in the singing night you come to me

Like some deep ocean-dream, with loosened hair

And once again I see your lighted eye,

Your soul's white miracle all naked-fair.

I write your golden name on golden sands

And watch the fing'ring waves smooth it away

To quiet oblivion with their froth-white hands;

But in my heart your name outlives their way.

Nocturne and Awakening

After the blare of cities, peace;

After the fanfare of men's voices, quiet;

Quiet and the soaring amplitude of song,

With you to fill the dusk with incense,

You to weave deep fugues of feeling

While I fold you, kneeling…kneeling.

I know how Beauty, youth-enchanted and asleep,

Must wake to passion's high ennoblement,

To learn her body's white astonishment,

Her miracle of lovely lucid flesh;

And feel those gently stirring giants, Sense and Touch,

That sound their drums along swift leagues of blood,

And stream the banners of delirium in your face,

Sweeping dumb centuries into a moment's flood;

Deserting cloisters dim for Love's resurgent earth

To blow dream-trumpets in the palaces of birth.

Prelude

1.

Now silence and your vacant chair keep tryst,

Your chair where many a pensive night you sank

After the million-pointed frets of day

Had charged upon your tenderness—and there,

A step away, the piano that you loved;

Where you would sit in halcyon hours of peace

Fingering old memory into sonant dream....

How could I, oh how could I know, the while

You spun your swift and silver-threaded themes,

And launched with glancing sails your argosy of dreams

On Jason-quests to find some unimagined Golden Fleece,

How could I know the dayspring of our love

Would sweep, dark flood on flood, to this far-plunging close?

And later, like a drift of darkness, soft you leaned

To brood upon the silver fall of ash and shooting spark.

I stood by you and stooped to brush my mouth upon

Your crimson rose, its hundred dewy-cluster'd lips a-glow.

You said, amazingly, "Love is the spirit's ladder'd fire to heaven."

And then a silence, pushed aside like curtains

With a wonder-breath of lovely, cryptic words:

"All shadow is the darkened memory of light,

And sorrow brings the enlightened soul to flight."

Time and your loss have coined your deepest meaning.

And then upon a fainting day you swept into the room;

Now Memory's a dying rose upon a dead nun's tomb.

2.

Time breaks proud lances with the hearts of men,

And Grief and Death stand victors at the fall;

Grief huddled with his scalding bowl of tears,

Death towering with his dagger buried deep.

Reflections of an Un-Naturalist
The Crossbill

In Nature's script of wit sardonic

The crossbill's case is sadly chronic

How does he feed

Or crack a seed

With one bill East

And one bill West?

To add disaster to confusion

With logic shattered in perfusion,

When Jill sets out to find her Bilbo

Her future mate must be a crossbeau.

Requiem for F.R.H.
(After Tagore)

I know a time will come, a day, an hour,

When every skill, all tears, all prayers—

Even the last dear talisman of love—

All, all will fail….

She is gone, the dunelight of my heart,

For the voice of the great wind has called her;

The far stars leaned down and spoke from the
     infinite spaces,

and the deeps rolled their thunder, saying:

"Go! Fly from these shores; bruise yourself no
     longer on these stones,

for your debt is paid, the forfeit rendered.

You have won your kingdom.

Let peace fill the place that has known you;

Let love and song enfold the memories you leave behind;

Let joy touch the dayspring of another day."

(1981)

Song

There floats a lilt of song
Within my heart;
I cannot tell how long
Ere it depart.

A name I found so sweet
My lips to frame;
Ah, sweetest things are fleet
When turned to shame!

I leaned so close to heed
Love's whisp'ring lips
And now I find no need
For Jason's ships!

My heart has found its home
And pain must cease;
No more dark seas I'll roam
For a Golden Fleece!

(October 28, 1930)

To Vilda

You smile at me with elfin grace,

Your dark eyes dancing with delight;

Oh, may you never learn to trace

My aching pity for your plight.

You cannot know, dear little one,

The anguish of the voided heart:

The voided heart, the love that's gone,

The broken lights…the tears…the smart.

Nor can you ever understand

Who takes sweet joy in everything,

Why I, who watch Time's running sand

Because of you can scarcely sing!

Poor little bud, you may not burst

Into your summer's radiant bloom,

But lie there with a hidden thirst

For flowerings that may never come.

Some day your eyes will wonder why

You are not just as others be;

I know that then you'll surely cry

For that will be…reality!

(Seattle, March 26, 1931)

To A Baby, Growing

Dear me! Whence all this elfin chatter,

Fraught with wanton wordless wit;

Floating from the wide-flung shutter

Dainty, impish, exquisite!

What! Storming at Life's tripled corslet

With your conquering gnomish lance:

Trilling each soft-gurgling driblet

In your pigmy puissance?

Tinkling, dream-light angel laughter

Chiming on two rosy lips:

Crimson-bannered's baby psalter

Stored with psalms in mystic scripts!

Stay, stay, you silver-singing scamp!

Whence, oh whence, that dreadful wrath?

Are you sailing galleons damp

In your soapy, scented bath?

Song for Music
(On Puget Sound)

The sunlight slants upon the sea,
The waves cream on the shore,
And soft winds breathe a melody
Of ancient, tongueless lore.

Along the strand the sifting dunes
Are stealing with the wind,
And myriad-tongued they chant the runes
No magic e'er may find.

In convoluted sorcery
Of ocean-crooning shells,
Deep rolls the muted litany
Of Time-eclipsing swells.

Sonnet

1.

Grace crowns your beauty's templed loveliness—
A magic fane for miracle and dream;
And flames, as once it flamed of old in theme
Of sword-embattled story, when redress
Of blood was stolen Beauty's dear largess.

2.

To a Photograph

Sweet face, sweet shadowed haunt of sister flowers,
The violet, lily, and the blushful rose,
Why, pray, that pensive smile, if not to gloze
Rare thoughts that lie enchained 'mid golden bowers?
What passionate intrigue of Love's fragrant hours
Implores that downward glance? Can it disclose
How violets do obeisance to the rose,
Bowing, life-thrilled, before Life's untried powers?

Conscript am I to the spell of those dear eyes,

Whose witchery bends my soul into the whirl

Of heavenward-rushing spirits in the skies.

Awake, thy voice, enchanting minstrel-girl,

And blow Love's own sweet Oliphant; Ah, fill

My cup of passion at thy lips' pure rill.

Sonnet

To----

I who have loved you now these many days

Have learned the anguish of deep ecstasy,

The spirit's counsel, soul's proud equity,

With the lifting rapture of our love's high praise.

What though there be some shriven ghost of song

Within our hearts?—One singing pulsing tone

Outsoars all fear, all doubt—great carillon

Of love's supreme indenture with the strong!

I knew that love ran like a golden seam

Through Homer's song, and wove a rare device

In Vergil's line; while in Dante's mighty dream

Love shaped a Paradise—for Beatrice!

For me these visions hold no dear surcease;

Your heart, your hands, your eye for me were peace!

Sonnet

To Beauty

I have sought Beauty where the tiger hurls
His grim apocalypse of tooth and claw;
Where Hunger runs on padded feet to draw
A blood-diced lottery with Death; where twirls
The nautch-girl's dance to cymbal and to song
While templed Shiva weaves dark looms of shame;
Where plangent rivers run with banks aflame
And down the dim night swoons the golden gong.

Sublime above the frenzied haunts of men,
O Beauty, you have swept the passionate heart
To seize the magic dream with brush and pen,
Win form from stone and sound in deathless art.
In the unweeting dark of life you came,
The benediction in the beating flame!

(1975)

Spring Nocturne In Seattle

When cats roam in the voiceless dark
On scientific quest
I oft on war's grim path embark
With swift, impassioned zest.

What though the night be gashed with noise,
What though it sprout keen claw,
Or the footless glooms horrific joys
Boast neither rhyme nor law?

For cats like lamp-eyed comets sail
Through skylight and through park,
And bright-haired co-eds lie and quail
Or start up terror-stark!

When shrilling obligatos soar
And ribboned fur runs red,
The night air sings with jagged things
From windows overhead.

Yet underneath the reign of stars

'Tis sweet to hear the din,

And consecrate the night to Mars

With a rain of empty tin!

Spring Nostalgia

In the spring an old man's fancy

Dreams again of valiant youth,

Yearning for some necromancy

Whereby Time may gloss the truth.

Ah, come again, dear radiant days

When nothing in the world was old,

When every storm shot silver sprays

And every vista spun with gold!

Then the minutes trudged like hours,

Now the hours flash by like minutes;

Youth sets no measure to its powers;

Age learns, alas, its flagging limits.

(February, 1976)

Spring Song

Blue gossamer of thought,

Gold gossamer of dream,

Webbed for your dancing-veil

Spun without seam.

Spring for your timbrel

With shaken bells ringing—

Bird-notes like silver coins

Rain for your singing!

Spume-white your body,

O sun-girl light flashing—

Spin your dew-patterns,

Your sun-hair cascading!

When come the cloud shadows

And slow weaves the dance,

Make love your enfolding

To hold you in trance!

Strictly Academic

You sit across your shining desk
And smoothly prate of Truth
As though it were some tinseled toy,
Some bauble meant for youth.

You smile elaborate scorn at me,
As patiently, apart,
I fumble with the delicate
Deep secrets of my heart.

I fear your nice moralities
That crush to finest dust
The chalice of my sanctities
So grimly won, so just.

Summer Treasure

I have seen bees, deep from the painted cups

Of flowers,

Steal away on busy wing

Heavy with the gold lore of scented gardens.

I have seen dim pools, hewn from the marble of

Gigantic silence,

Dark, marmoreal, tranced…

Where Beauty's self doth kiss her mirror'd face.

I have looked deep into a woman's eyes

Coy, chatoyant, poised,

And mingled with the hoardings of her gold years.

I, who have graved with iron stylus on the flint of Time.

The Brownies

They creep from out among the trees
To yawn and rub their eyes,
Then wash their hands in silver dew
Beneath the starry skies.

They bring their tiny babies too,
Each in a moth-wing quilt,
Then feed them milk from acorn cups,
Nor ever a drop is spilt.

All night the Brownies dance and sing
And run in elfin race;
With hands joined in a fairy ring
They skip with elfin grace.

But when the hills are touched with gold,
These lovely little gnomes
Soon creep in ones and twos and threes
Back to their secret homes.

You never see the Brownies play

Before the sun has set;

But when the shadows come to stay

They on the lawn have met.

The Graduate

1.

But look, oh look, who now comes by,

This Hector of the fishy eye,

Homeric tread, Cimmerian frown,

The Senior!—sybarite of cap and gown!

Hero of a thousand quizzes,

Quaffer of uncounted fizzes—

This Trigger-happy little chappy

Kneads the dough sent by his pappy.

2.

Four years he's dwelt in sun and bower

Ducking an intellectual shower—

This Lucifer of fallen arches,

This Grendel of the midnight marches.

Ah soon, too soon will come Tomorrow—

That's mare's-nest filled with eggs of sorrow

A traveler in the realms of gold,

<u>This</u> rolling stone has gathered mold.

The Gobbler's Lament
(For Thanksgiving)

From Plymouth Rock to Arkansas

We're birds of high tradition;

We've served you well through freeze and thaw

To succulent perdition.

Where once we skimmed through sunlit woods,

A flashing dream of color,

Today we herd in flightless broods

In treeless, muddy squalor.

With blood-red banners flaunting high,

We're fattened for the kill;

With brilliant eye and never a cry

We meet our Bunker Hill.

We gobble early, gobble late

(I don't mean only food);

We bravely bear our 'seasoned' fate,

A doomed and feathered brood.

Our fate is sealed from birth to death;

Our destiny: to serve,

Our karma bound in every breath,

We give without reserve.

While constellations endless turn,

<u>We</u> turn on spit and grill,

And at your feast, while candles burn,

The nation's prayers fulfill.

The Last Avatar
(of Vishnu)

With grey messiahs nailed upon a cross,

Let us be done! Grim conscripts of the Lost,

We prime our missiles for the holocaust,

Our dry hearts bankrupt, leprous with the moss

Of lies and hate, of green and envy, dross

Of bitter pride.... No fires of Pentecost

For us, no Second Coming. All is frost

And bleak beyond our night's abysmal loss.

The Nothing Book Speaks:

I'm laughing as you riffle through my empty pages

Intent on finding here the Wisdom of the Ages.

Though nothing here to read, there's much to ruminate;

The lore of nothingness I'll now elucidate:

The flute, the trombone, horn is each an empty tube.

Just try to con sweet music from a rod, you boob!

A wheel, to spin, must have an empty center space;

A house without a window is a sightless face.

Because of empty space man writes his signature

On moon, on Venus, Mars—heaven's red entablature!

But should you smarm your gal with empty compliment,

You'll surely earn, my friend, her shrewdest punishment!

Two things abhorred by Nature, I must you remind:

A vacuum, and the blankness of an empty mind!

The Prisoner

Darkly caught in subtlest mesh,

Prisoned in your fainting flesh,

I have seen you shake your bars,

Desperate, once, to reach the stars.

Prometheus bound to a rock,

Chained for gods and men to mock.

What writhing horror makes you swoon

And pray for Death's triumphant boon?

Behind your bitter charm of face,

Beneath your body's riven grace,

Will this grapple never end?

Will you spirit never bend?

But sometimes, sudden in the mirror,

Staring, cringing, drenched with terror,

Broken hands strike giant bars,

Desperate, once, to climb the stars!

The Woman Speaks

I meet you now, I, the true Woman

Who was bitter and dying in the strike;

From depth upon depth of blue darkness

I have won back, have won back to Life!

I have sped to the surface for breathing,

Like a diver released from the fight,

From the ravening horror—the Formless;

The squid-murk, the nightmare, the Night!

I have leapt at your fashioning touch

From the central gloom-chambers of Death…

I have stirred like the angel-touched waters

And brimmed back to fountain-bright life.

I have burst—unwreathed like a flower!

In the sunlight, the morning's rose-flushing;

Swift earth-sap, exultant, mounts arrowy,

Triumphant, delirious, aflame!

I am couched, I am couched like a flower,

All waiting, all radiant, a spangle of dew-glint

A-glimmer—a burning bright chalice

For the wine-sap of love and of life!

To the Little Mite

When my Little Mite comes home to roos'
She first must drink her orange juice;
Then sponge her wayward waxen thighs
Ere she a coffin-nail espies!

Don't let her sit with hellish brood
Of 'wayward imps' and horrid dreams,
But creep between the new-laid sheets
And in her dreams write reams and reams!

Ultima Thule

When the last beastly grade-sheet is entered
   And you've boosted that C-plus to B,
Or you bite at your pen again, frowning,
   At that sudden recalcitrant D,

Then scrap every book, pen and pencil,
   On classroom and desk turn your back:
Burn every damned blue-book and stencil—
   For the English Prof's off on his vac!

Then the tide is an undulant egg-flip
   That is whipped by the knife-keen breeze,
And you bluster about in you bath-suit,
   Or cower by the pier, and sneeze.

Now poems are word-candied lightnings
   And the sun is an orange-bright peel;
The stars, like girl-clusters in heaven,
   Slyly wink, nudge each other, and squeal.

Come lounge on far rims of existence,

Mount the gold-patinaed carpet of Time;

Let the thunder's dim distant quiescence

Sound the drum-roll of battles sublime!

What's In A Name?

I've read of men in high estate,

Of kind, and queen, and Rajah

But now of late there's hot debate

For what, oh <u>what</u>, is Tajah?

I've heard of jeweled Taj Mahal,

Of harp-loud halls of Tara,

And tales Ashurbanipal,

But where, oh <u>where</u> is Tajah?

I've drunk my fill at tinkling rill,

To the bitter wells of Marah;

But all is tranquil, all is still,

The desert wind sighs "Tajah!"

I've given odds to all the gods,

And even offered poojah*;

No word, no answer give those sods

To <u>what</u>, or <u>where</u> is Tajah.

Since Tajah answers not to *what,*

Nor to the question *where,*

My temper fast is going to pot—

I 'm tearing out my hair!

Now startling news from Ind bring hint

To lay all vexing rumor:

That Tajah is a saucy kind**

Self-named, self-styled—with humor!

*Hindi–prayer,

**German–child

Wood

Beech wood fires are bright and clear
If the logs are kept a year,
Chestnut's only good, they say,
If for long it's laid away.
Birch and fir logs burn too fast,
Blaze up bright and do not last,
It is by the Irish said.
Hawthorne bakes the sweetest bread
Elm wood burns like a church yard mold,
E'en the very flames are cold.
Poplar gives a bitter smoke,
Fills your eyes and makes you choke.
Apple wood will scent your room
With an incense-like perfume.
Oaken logs, if dry and old,
Keep away the winter cold.
But ash wood wet and ash wood dry,
A king shall warm his slippers by.

*Limericks, One-Liners
And Other Nonsense*

It often happens that the simplest actions of a person, when looked at through a haze of fear or jealousy, may appear to proceed from the depths of cunning.

The highest form of altruism is self-cultivation.

His job canonical; his tongue thrasonical.

In America men's clothes are cut to flatter what they haven't got, while women's clothes snicker 'roundly' at what they have.

How could he be stoic with problem entozoic?

I have finally reached an age (87) when the more austere strictures of monasticism have finally become the idioms of nature, against which there can be no appeal.

Life is often prodigal with the destruction of excellence.

To read only newspapers is to keep one forever on the mad crossings of life. To read only magazines is like passing acquaintances at a party. But to read great books is to gather with old friends round the fire for great talk and splendid laughter.

It is curious how so many women drift into the habit of dribbling verbosity, a kind of enuresis of the mind. Very few have the gift of making silence as vindictive as speech.

Now we are told that matrimony prolongs life. But does not that depend somewhat upon the woman's aim?

How oft do friendly eyes deck dross with excellence....

The atom tongues the universe. A word can topple kings.

He pursed up his lips like the tightened mouth of a dufflebag.

The Pursuit-of-Truth syndrome often develops into a ritual purgation by orgy.

To give rumor the rind of credibility.

Having drawn a little blood, she retracts her claws and purrs again.

He uses irony as an emotional styptic.

History is nothing but the extended dreams of the fly caught forever in the cruel amber.

History is what enables each nation to use the other fellow's past record as an alibi.

The man who boasts of having 'an open mind' often mistakes a vacancy for an opening.

In a day when the term "modernism" finds so protean a set of definitions, it is more gracious to be labeled 'sane' than 'modern'.

The unhappiest man is the one whose expenditure of speech is too great for his income of ideas.

Cleverness is merely an intellectual itch on the scrofulous skin of mediocrity.

Two styles of writing: A nude woman leaves nothing to the imagination, yet one is never in doubt as to her form and texture. But an overdressed woman leaves everything to the imagination and nothing to good taste.

Some prose writers go from bad to verse.

English composition is the only subject in which one cannot afford to have all the virtues of theory without some of the vices of practice.

We must read only of those great lives that have pinnacled themselves in history. And we, standing upon the bracing summits of their achievements, shade our eyes and descry the distant adventure of new horizons.

A great painting is often created like a great poem; for the great fundamental idea or the actuating principle of each is really a composite of innumerable moods—a splendid mosaic of exquisite little passions.

Our thoughts and acts are like a sculptor's fingers that either ruthlessly shatter the formless clay of our spirits, or with patient and skilled diligence mould a glorious monument for the future.

There are men who go straight to Hell while gazing into the eyes of God.

That man is a fool who makes of his personal religion a mere paragraph of words.

Unbelief is really not so much a denial or a negation as a blindness; it is Credulity and Intelligence lashed across the eyes with the Whip of Experience.

We lift our hands to thee, oh Lord, and swing the smoking censers of imagination about the secret altars of our heart, as our thoughts move to thee in the great silent processional of eternal litanies.

So many of our most cherished memories are guarded by the frozen and eternal vigil of salt pillars, terrible in their blind, mute search for the lost glories of old days.

In every effort at personal revision we are brought face to face with the problem that brought Lot's wife into history.

It's an ironic fact in life that the less you know the ropes, the more certain are you of being in the noose.

Definite conclusions are usually safe blind alleys of the logical intelligence.

To lack a sense of convention is the highest form of conventionality.

Satisfaction is a sloth that feeds on discontent.

Tradition enjoys a lone immunity from the scourge of orthodoxy.

In America, patriotism is the tribute pride pays to disloyalty.

In America life is a continual routine of feeding the fishes of Democracy with the undigested delicacies of culture.

I am a man of few words, mostly long ones.

The greatest works of art are those that achieve the transcendent without losing the heartbeat of simplicity.

The compensations of insight sometimes strike a perilous balance with the horrors of discovery.

This morning I saw a radioactive bird sitting on a nuclear twig, fairly exploding with atomic music.

Love consists in this: That two solitudes protect, and touch, and greet each other.

When the floods come up, the fish eat ants. When the floods go down, the ants eat fish.

I am afraid that, for some of us, the areas of necessity have expanded to narrow the margins of more gracious indulgence.

By his exclusions, the artist creates a work of art. But by the same process of exclusion, the critic defines his own limitations.

One longs especially to smash the fatuous creed that conceives of God as a sort of divine confectioner, manufacturing saintly sugar-plums for the virtuous and secretly preparing a cauldron of boiling oil for all the damned doughnuts of this world.

A 'dirty old man' is one whose libido fails to underwrite the investment promise of a roving eye.

A pest is a creature who forces license upon opportunity.

The cynic is usually one who is afraid that life will prick some of the exquisite bubbles of his vanity.

Mediocrity is life cast in the plain idiom of a job-trot. Cleverness is life flashing into a mechanical brilliance. But Genius is life caught in the fluent movements of higher rhythms, flying with free rein and the splendid spur!

In the individual it is possible for art and life to be unified in a beautiful stability by a fusion of moral and aesthetic values. Such a coalition points most surely to spiritual expansion.

Skepticism is very often the fear of belief.

There is no sense in loving someone you can never wake up to except by chance.

When a man talks of one woman to another he usually brings about that condition in nature known as a 'short circuit'—HE is the blown fuse!

I think now that being free is being able to love. To love someone else enough to forget about yourself even for one moment is to be free.

Our desire for another will lift us out of ourselves more cleanly than anything divine.

I know, too, that without love, we grope the tunnels of our lives and never see the sun.

In America, marriage is the only public institution that indulges no private grudge against the economy of the moment.

The blind positivism of weak natures is really the terror of earning general disbelief.

Marriage is the eternal apology common sense owes romance.

Obsession plus love decreases at such and such a rate per year of separation, squared by distance, until even the strongest of previous attachments have achieved a certain entropic quantity, a formulaic numbness, a death.

If the love between a man and woman is to endure, it is of the gravest importance that each possess some ultimate little Holy Grail of the spirit that will be the object of eternal quest for the other.

She is a woman who uses nostalgia as a flagellant, wounding herself with the twin whips of regret and remorse.

I am heartily glad that the vast cornucopia of Christmas business has ceased pouring its chromium-and-tinsel bounty upon the milling urban herds of sheep who have by now been well fleeced in a spectacle that does dishonor to the human spirit.

It often happens that a wordless exemplar outshines a babbling messiah.

How easy it is to impute evil to another's reactions to a set of circumstances, to which you stand a total stranger. The imputation of evil is the safety valve used by Ignorance and Fear to reduce the unpleasant pressure of Truth.

People always want to make an equal exchange of Gethsemane for heaven; but they forget that the toll gate is Golgotha.

Life's aspic has turned into a Molotov cocktail.

Death has no habit of elegance, and in the last of life's wardrobes, there are no disguises.

Her beauty was at that turning point when artificial embellishment no longer enhances natural charm, but merely becomes what it is—the ineffectual mark for a futile deception through which peers a terrified soul.

In the long arithmetic of human experience, there are many recurring decimals.

In the long run, a harmful truth is better than a useful lie.

Graffiti (January, 1976)

You whom on this pot now sit

With nothing more in mind than sh--,

Now draw, like any piggish runt

Crude pictures wild of cock and cunt.

Added to verses on a Christmas card to Glen and Charlotte for Christmas, 1975:

Through jaundiced sun and buck-shot rain,

Through murder, mayhem, crime,

My golden thoughts fly straight to you

On the wings of Christmas chime!

Sent to Charlene in a box of hulwa, Christmas, 1975:

You swear that sparingly you eat,

And vow your heart is chaste.

Behold—all vows in full retreat

When you this hulwa taste.

Worry

Let worry worry trifles

And it will just be this,

That trifling worry rifles

Your little world of bliss.

Retort Curt-eous

You say my hide is very thick,

My head, you say, is hard,

But when I look at you, my friend

Behold—A tub of lard.

Miss Snyder

I once knew a wench named Miss Snyder,

Whose neighbors could hardly abide her,

"She's so damnably snide,"

In a chorus they cried,

"With hard cider Miss Snyder's still snider!"

Beezlepuss

Old Beezlepuss lived in a grotto;

His life-long obsession was Lotto.

Far and wide spread his fame

As he lost every game

For he only played Lotto when blotto!

Amrita

A ravenous goat was Amrita,

Whose master, a pundit, would beat her.

But she soon had HIM beaten

When he found she had eaten

The whole of his Bhagaved Gita!

A Christmas Toast

Since twice a thousand bloody years

Have spooked our Christmas cheer

Let's drink, in flagons brimmed with guilt,

To Hate, and Greed, and Fear!

Animals

The camel is a graceful bird

That flits from tree to tree

And light on a black lizard

Is stung by a bumble bee.

The gavial though a surly croc

Is friendly in a crunch,

And freely gives you gator-aid,

When serving you for lunch.

Marriage

It has been said of married bliss

That love dies out from kiss to kiss.

Can this be true

Of me and you?

For forty years your lips divine

Have kept distilling heady wine

To pledge life's banquet, rain or shine.

Epigram

No man may cross his Rubicon,

Then think to hurry back;

For once committed, if he turn,

His foes will stab and hack.

Acknowledgements

There are many people to thank for the compilation of this book. Of course, the first goes to my father, the author of all stories, poems, one-liners and other shorts herein. Had he and his second family not welcomed me back into their family, this never would have happened. My two brothers, Trog (Glen Jr.) and Trevor Harris provided details for the biography, as well as Laura Ware, daughter of Ramsay Harris, Jr. She was also kind enough to critique the whole Introduction from the writing standpoint as well as the information. Ana Ware June, Laura's daughter, a writer in her own stead, supplied details about the transition from Burma to Colgate University in upstate New York.

My thanks to Karla Tofte, Peter Kelley, Elliott Stevens and J.D, Bolcer from the University of Washington for their assistance with the prior publications of the author's work in their publications. Regrettably, I cannot find the name of the nice lady, the administrative assistant at Colgate University, who aided me with the same assistance in their own publication, *The Willow Path*. My thanks also to Claudia Keelan of *Interim*, for her help with that publication.

My thanks, too, to members of the writers' groups who gave me their suggestions and critiques of my Introduction: Debbie Cooper, April Ryan, Cheryl Vezetinski, Janice Van Cleve and Sheila Sidan.

I may have inadvertently left out someone, and if I have, please forgive me. It was certainly not intentional.

Cover Biography

Glen Harris began writing in his late teens while at Rangoon College in Burma. His love of words and language grew and flourished at Colgate University, where he published short pieces in *The Willow Path*, Colgate's literary magazine. He also published in *Month's Best,* a University of Washington publication, when he taught there, as well as in *Interim*, a literary magazine then based in Seattle. Although his teaching career ended, he continued to write for his own benefit and fun well into retirement. The stories, poems and other short writings presented here are all of the completed works we have found. He finished out his life in retirement still in Seattle. His final six years were spent in a nursing home, with a mind very much intact, but a body which had ceased to accommodate his needs for independent living. At age 107, he declared, "A pox on it!" and shuffled off this mortal coil.

www.ingramcontent.com/pod-product-compliance
Lightning Source LLC
Chambersburg PA
CBHW030149100526
44592CB00009B/198